**ABOUT THE FRONT COVER**

*"It is a long road and sunny,*
*It's a long road and old,*
*And the brown padres made it,*
*For the flocks of the fold."*
Frank S. Jones, "The Long Road," *History of Decatur County, Georgia*

This photograph was taken in 2013 while driving down the Bellamy Road in Alachua County. Passing by this side farm road on my right, I did an abrupt stop and reversed my SUV. There I beheld a trail that resembled, more than anything I had ever seen, what I envisioned as the Spanish Trail. I had no idea at the time that this was in fact the old trail, but I took the photo anyway. Later I determined that this may not only be the old trail, but was near the site of the Timucuan village of Malapaz, and the possible Santa Fe Trail from the south that Hernando de Soto traveled. Look into the tops of the trees, and find the ghost of an old padre hovering there.

# THE SPANISH ROAD

**TRAVELS ALONG FLORIDA'S ROYAL ROAD, EL CAMINO REAL**

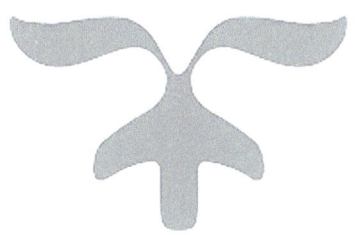

**BY ROBERT R. HURST**

**COPYRIGHT 2021** Robert R. Hurst
The Spanish Road

Published by Yawn Publishing LLC
2555 Marietta Hwy, Ste 103
Canton, GA 30114
www.yawnspublishing.com

All rights reserved. No part of this book may be reproduced or transmitted in any form, electronic or mechanical, including photocopying, recording, or data storage systems without express written permission of the publisher, except for brief quotations in reviews or articles. This book is printed exactly as the author intended, without editorial input or reference verification from Yawn Publishing LLC.

Library of Congress Control Number:2021900423

ISBN:978-1-954617-01-8

Printed in the United States of America

## DEDICATION

*This work is dedicated to my high school American history teacher, David Lewis, who led me "down the path of history".*

# Table of Contents

Quote from Captain Hugh Young ................................................................. 11

Foreword ........................................................................................................ 13

Acknowledgements ........................................................................................ 15

List of Figures ................................................................................................ 17

Preface ............................................................................................................ 21

      The Mission Road ............................................................................. 22

      Jackson's Trail ................................................................................... 24

Author's Note ................................................................................................ 25

**1.** Saint Augustine ...................................................................................... 27

**2.** The Picolata Path .................................................................................... 29

**3.** The San Pedro Path ................................................................................ 41

**4.** The Old Field Path ................................................................................. 45

**5.** The Center Path ...................................................................................... 49

**6.** The Road through Georgia ..................................................................... 55

**7.** The Road to Sabacola ............................................................................. 59

**8.** The Road to Calistoble .......................................................................... 61

**9.** The Red Ground Path ............................................................................. 67

**10.** The Lower Creek Trading Path ............................................................ 73

**11.** The End of the Trail ............................................................................. 81

**Appendix I:** Points of Interest ................................................................... 83

**Appendix II:** Auto and Hiking Tours ........................................................ 85

**Appendix III:** Places & Roads along the Spanish Trail from St. Augustine to Pensacola .... 87

Bibliography .................................................................................................. 89

Index .............................................................................................................. 91

*" ... a line of works was extended from Little River to St. Augustine running nearly in an east and west direction and connected by a broad highway (Fig. 1), made practicable through the lower parts of the country by durable causeways and bridges. At each of the points where the population rendered a fortification necessary a work was regularly constructed. Generally on a square, with bastions and a rampart and parapet of earth...in order - Little River, St. Rose at Okalokina [Ochlocknee River] - a fort on Assilla [Aucilla River] - St. Pedro on Histenhatchee and St. Francisco on St. Juan's [Suwannee River]. The highway connecting these different settlements is yet to be seen in many places where the Indian routes through the country cross or run along with it. The upper Sahwanne [Suwannee] path is parallel with the great road for a considerable distance and one of its forks is crossed by the [Lower] path from St. Marks to Assilla. The deep indentations in the soil will preserve the road visible for centuries. At the crossing place of Assilla Creek, the remains of a bridge and extensive causeway of cabbage tree logs evidence the industry of the Spaniards and the population of their settlements at a former day."* [1]

Captain Hugh Young with General Andrew Jackson's army, 1818

Figure 1: The "Broad Highway", Little River Springs Conservation Area, Suwannee Co.

---

[1] Captn. Hugh Young, "A Topographical Memoir on East and West Florida with Itineraries of General Jackson's Army, 1818", *Florida Historical Quarterly* 13, no. 2 (Oct. 1934): 98.

# Forward

*"Historic trails were considered important, since it is assumed that deSoto's army did not wander across a trackless wilderness, but followed established pathways. Such trails, [noted Florida archaeologist Louis] Tesar reasoned, would continue to be used well into the historic period."*

Ewen and Hann, 1998[2]

The course of the roads described in this work has heavily relied upon the early maps of the Spanish, British, and Americans. This is especially true of the pre-territorial Florida map by Joseph Purcell entitled *Map of the Road from Pensacola in West Florida to St. Augustine in East Florida*. The assumption has been made that these roads of the Spanish period may have continued in service during the early American occupation of the 1820's and beyond. Therefore, nineteenth century U. S. maps and early aerial photographs of the late 1930's and into the 1940's have been searched for vestiges of the earlier roads. Among the most valuable are the early U. S. survey maps that date as early as 1824. They are surprisingly accurate. They have been most useful in those parts of the trail from the St. Johns River to the Tallahassee area, where some of the roads labelled "St. Augustine Road", "Federal Road", and "Bellamy Road" are in the footprint of the Spanish Road. Also, they have been useful in the west where the road is labelled "General Jackson's Trail" (Fig. 2 & 3).

While it is quite true that the Spanish Roads are inextricably tied to the Franciscan mission development across Florida, they did not evolve so much by the location of the missions than they did by the location of the pre-existing Native American paths. Communication with the missions necessitated their maintenance and improvement, but not necessarily their direction. It can also be said that the precursory Indian trails evolved, not only from the settlement pattern, but, as importantly, from the topography of the land. The "path of least resistance" rule applied here. Ridges, basin divides, river fords, and natural bridges were on the preferred route. Roads were not straight, but curved with the contour of the land. Therefore, the topography of the land has influenced the tracings of these roads herein described.

Then there are the journals kept by the travelers along the Spanish Road. The Spanish narrators include the Catholic Bishop Gabriel Diaz Vara Calderon, Deputy Governor Juan Fernandez de Florencia, soldier and rancher Marcos Delgado, Captain Don Lorenzo de Tores y Ayala, Friar Rodrigo de la Barreda, and Lieutenant Diego Pena. The British expedition of 1778 resulted in the journal of Captain David Holmes and the itinerary and

---

[2] Charles R. Ewen & John H. Hann, *Hernando de Soto among the Apalachee: The Archaeology of the First Winter Encampment*, (Gainesville: University Press of Florida, 1998), 14.

the map commentaries of the cartographer Joseph Purcell. Finally, there is the commentary and chronicle of Captain Hugh Young, who reported on General Andrew Jackson's march in 1818.

The most useful of these are the journals of Ayala and Pena for the western and eastern portion of the road, respectively, and the journal of Young for the western portion and the itinerary of Purcell for the 18th century road. Young's measurements, then Purcell's, both of which are given in miles, are the most accurate. The Spanish travelers measured in leagues and they sometimes conflict with each other and with those given in miles by the British and Americans.

Lastly, there have been site inspections. Much of the road has been driven or hiked where possible. Photographic documentation has been made on all parts of the road.

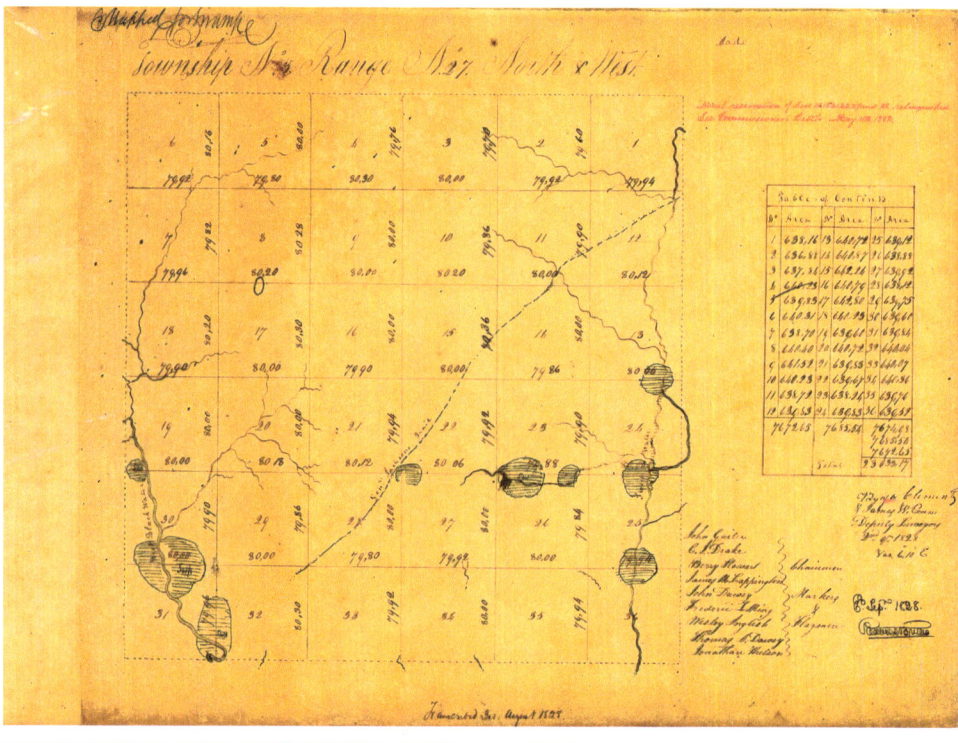

(Top) Figure 2: 1828 U. S. Survey map of Township 3N, Range 27W, showing "Gen'l Jacksons Trail"

(Bottom) Figure 3: Portion of I. G. Searcy's 1829 *Map of Florida*, showing "Jackson's Trail". Courtesy Library of Congress.

# Acknowledgements

I suppose that I am no different from any other writer or researcher or actor and actress for that matter. In making acknowledgements, there is always the concern of omitting someone from the recognition that he or she deserves. Despite this fear, it seems only appropriate to attempt it. So here are my partners, companions, and mentors in no particular order.

**Dr. Joe Barnett and Mark Dick**, both of Tallahassee, for their companionship and help in tracing the path, especially along the Suwannee River and its springs.

**Rebecca Saunders,** my childhood friend and librarian (now retired), for her help with my research.

**Tom Bowen,** with the DOT in Chipley, for partnering with me on so much of this research.

**Dean DeBolt**, librarian, and **Dr. Brian Rucker,** both of Pensacola, and **Peter Cowdrey** of Tallahassee for advice, encouragement and help.

**Lynn Mangum** of Tallahassee, for introducing me to so much of the Spanish mission period, and for her encouragement to pursue this project.

**Bob Daffin,** my childhood friend, for his companionship on my trips to various sites.

**Sam Carnley** and historian **Dale Cox** for their help with Jackson County roads and missions.

**David Fowler** and **Sharman Ramsey,** authors, for all the help and advice on formatting and publishing my book.

**Mark Hendrick** for the graphic design of the book.
(All photographs are in the collection of R. Hurst except where indicated)

# List of Figures

**Figure 1:** The "Broad Highway", Little River Springs Conservation Area, Suwannee Co. ................................................................................................. 11

**Figure 2:** 1828 U. S. Survey map of Township 3N, Range 27W, showing "Gen'l Jacksons Trail" ................................................................................. 14

**Figure 3:** Portion of I. G. Searcy's *1829 Map of Florida*, showing "Jackson's Trail". Courtesy Library of Congress............................................. 14

**Figure 4:** El Camino Real Historic Marker, Bainbridge..................................... 21

**Figure 5:** The Long Road: "It's a long road and sunny, It's a long road and old, And the brown padres made it, For the flocks of the fold." Frank S. Jones, *History of Decatur County, Georgia.* ........................... 23

**Figure 6:** The Mission Road. "And lo! A light from heaven shown down. And I beheld through the briars, the Mission Road of the Franciscan Friars." Bob Hurst, April 6, 2013, Charles Spring, Suwannee Co........ 25

**Figure 7:** The City Gates, St. Augustine ca. 1861-1865. A view looking into town along St. Georges St. Courtesy Library Congress................. 27

**Figure 8:** Sam Rosworth's plan of St. Augustine's northern defense, 1765-1775, showing, from left to right, the inner defense or Cubo line, the middle defense or Hornworks with "Barrier Gate", the outer defense or "Spanish Line" with "Stockade Fort", nearby "Crossing Place", and "Mosey Fort". The Picolata Path is shown between the inner and middle defense lines and near the Stockade Fort. Rosworth was the British Surveyor General of Florida. Courtesy Library of Congress, Geography and Map Division.............. 28

**Figure 9:** Primitive road north of present Picolata Road, St. Johns Co. .............. 30

**Figure 10:** Second Seminole War Cemetery, Picolata........................................... 30

**Figure 11:** "On each side of the river…[is] a sentry box…, named respectively Pupe and Picolata…" St. Johns River looking south with Picolata on the distant left shore and Pupa and Bayard Point on the near right shore. Courtesy Florida History Online, University of North Florida............. 31

**Figure 12:** Portion of Joseph Purcell's *1778 Map of the Road from Pensacola in West Florida to St. Augustine in East Florida* showing the eastern segment of the Picolata Path from St. Augustine to Monteocha Creek in present Alachua Co. Courtesy National Archives, UK .......... 32

**Figure 13:** Bayard Road, Clay Co................................................................................ 33

**Figure 14:** A muddy Bellamy Road, Clay Co. .................................................... 34

**Figure 15:** Bellamy Road Historic Marker on US Highway 17, Clay Co. ............. 34

**Figure 16:** Portion of Joseph Purcell's *1778 Map of the Road from*

## LIST OF FIGURES

*Pensacola in West Florida to St. Augustine in East Florida,* showing the west segment of the Picolata Path and the San Pedro Path. Courtesy National Archives, UK .............................. 35

**Figure 17:** A Second Seminole War Map showing "Horse Trail" around the "Itoniah Scrub". Courtesy Library of Congress ................ 36

**Figure 18:** Private drive off Bellamy Road, Alachua Co. ....................................... 37

**Figure 19:** Paraner's Trail, Oleno State Park. ............................................................ 38

**Figure 20:** "The deep indentations in the soil will preserve the road visible for centuries." Dogwood Trail, Oleno State Park. ..................... 38

**Figure 21:** "Betwixt Seguana [Suwannee] and Santa Fe on each side of the path are many remarkable rocky springs ... " Baptizing Spring, Wes Skiles Peacock Springs State Park, Suwannee Co. ................................................................................................ 39

**Figure 22:** Charles Spring, Suwannee Co. ............................................................ 40

**Figure 23:** "I camped on the [other side of the] Rio de San Juan de Guacara [Suwannee River] ... I remained at this spot in order to rest the animals, which were much fatigued from swimming the river, which although not very wide, now has a strong current. It is about a pistol shot in width." Ezell's Landing on the Suwannee River, Lafayette Co. ........................................................... 42

**Figure 24:** Old St. Augustine Road, Madison Co. ................................................ 42

**Figure 25:** The tallest Indian mound in Florida. Letchworth-Love Mounds Archaeological State Park, Jefferson Co. ............................................. 46

**Figure 26:** Sunray Road, possibly atop the Spanish Road near the Miccosukee settlements, Leon Co. .................................................... 46

**Figure 27:** Portion of Joseph Purcell's 1778 *Map of the Road from Pensacola in West Florida to St. Augustine in East Florida,* showing the west segment of the San Pedro Path, the Old Field Path, and the east segment of the Road through Georgia. Courtesy National Archives, UK ......................................... 47

**Figure 28:** " ... old broad roads worn one, two and three feet deep ... plain and well trod." Deep cut (to left of fence) near US Highway 98 and Wadesboro Road, Tallahassee .................... 52

**Figure 29:** Old Bainbridge Road, Tallahassee. ...................................................... 53

**Figure 30:** " ... along old carriage roads worn one and two feet deep." Toole Dairy Road off Lake Douglas Road, Bainbridge. ...................... 56

**Figure 31:** Primitive road off Zorn Road, perhaps one of the few remains of the road in Georgia, West Bainbridge ............................. 56

**Figure 32:** Portion of Joseph Purcell's 1778 *Map of the Road from Pensacola in West Florida to St. Augustine in East Florida,* showing the west segment of the Road through Georgia, and the east segment of the Red Ground Path. Courtesy National Archives, UK ...................................................... 58

**Figure 33:** Segment of Vincente Sebastian Pintado's *Plano Borrador*

|  |  |
|---|---|
|  | *del limite comun a las dos Floridas y de los territories de ambas provincias adyacentes e el.*, ca. 1815. Courtesy Library of Congress ......................................................... 59 |
| **Figure 34:** | " ... on the road to Calistoble." Reddoch Road, Jackson Co. ............... 63 |
| **Figure 35:** | Old Spanish Trail interpretive sign and trace of the old road (right background), Blue Springs, Marianna. ............................ 63 |
| **Figure 36:** | Blue Springs with Robinson Plantation visible in distance, 1903. Courtesy of Florida Memory, Florida State Library & Archives................................................................................. 64 |
| **Figure 37:** | Beyond the Road to Calistoble. The Old Campbellton Road, north of the Union and Jacob Roads intersection, Jackson Co. ........... 66 |
| **Figure 38:** | Primitive road west of Choctawhatchee River and Curry Ferry, Holmes Co................................................................................................ 69 |
| **Figure 39:** | Andrew Jackson historical marker near Lake Jackson, Florala. ........... 70 |
| **Figure 40:** | Portion of Joseph Purcell's *1778 Map of the Road from Pensacola in West Florida to St. Augustine in East Florida*, showing the Lower Creek Trading Path and the west extremity of the Red Ground Path. Courtesy National Archives, UK ................................................................................ 71 |
| **Figure 41:** | "the path is plain and well trod." "General Jackson's Trail". East of Yellow River, Okaloosa Co. ..................................................... 74 |
| **Figure 42:** | Yellow River Baptist Church Road, Okaloosa Co............................... 75 |
| **Figure 43:** | Author Bob Hurst on the Jackson Trail, Blackwater River State Forest, Santa Rosa Co. ............................................................ 77 |
| **Figure 44:** | Primitive trail, Pace................................................................................ 79 |
| **Figure 45:** | The Picolata Path (marked in red) in Oleno State Park, Columbia Co.................................................................. 85 |
| **Figure 46:** | The Picolata Path (marked in red) in Little River Springs Conservation Area, Suwannee Co....................... 85 |
| **Figure 47:** | The Picolata Path (marked in red) in Wes Skiles Peacock Springs State Park, Suwannee Co........................ 86 |

# Preface

The year 2013 marked the 500th anniversary of Ponce de Leon's discovery of Florida and hence the beginning of Spanish influence in the state. As a result of this recognition, there has been a renewed interest in perhaps the most famous road in Florida's history, the Old Spanish Road. Few people realize that the road is not only part of Florida's history, but also of Alabama's and Georgia's. The only definitive map of the road was done in 1778 by an Englishman named Joseph Purcell, who actually traversed the road with British soldiers and Indians. Purcell's *Map of the Road from Pensacola in West Florida to St. Augustine in East Florida* was published in the *Florida Historical Quarterly* by the noted Florida Historian Mark Boyd, who remarked: "If any road through Florida might be called 'The Old Spanish Trail', it is this one."[3]

*"In communicating between Pensacola and St. Augustine ... the fords and ferries are scarcely ever practicable, and there are no accommodations, and scarcely inhabitants. The journey is performed by a circuitous route through Georgia and Alabama."*

Charles B. Vignoles, 1823[4]

Indeed, the trip was "circuitous", long, and arduous as will be illustrated as the reader follows the early travelers presented in this work. Purcell's group left Pensacola along a road that led them briefly into Alabama. Then they hugged the Florida/Alabama border, and then advanced into Georgia all the way to Bainbridge. The city actually has a state historic marker recognizing *El Camino Real,* "The Royal Road" (Fig. 4). Their travel then led them to the vicinity of Tallahassee and from there eastwards to Saint Augustine. It took their campaign 32½ marching days to traverse the total distance of 464 miles. Today the distance by modern roads is 367 miles and can be done in less than a day.

(Left) Figure 4: El Camino Real Historic Marker, Bainbridge

3. Mark F. Boyd, "A Map of the Road from Pensacola to St. Augustine, 1778", *Florida Historical Quarterly* 17, no. 1 (July 1938): 15.

4. Charles B. Vignoles, *Observations upon the Floridas* (New York: E. Bliss & E. White, 1823), 63.

The beginnings of the road are found in Saint Augustine, which was established in 1565. The Spanish needed a land route westwards for garrisoning troops, for quelling rebellions, and for repelling invasions; however more importantly, the history of The Spanish Road cannot be separated from the history of the development of the Spanish mission system.

Most scholars agree that the El Camino Real had expanded westwards from St. Augustine for about three leagues by 1600. One scholar dates the westward expansion as early as 1587.[5] By 1608, the road had been opened for three leagues west of the Aucilla river into Apalachee Indian territory.[6] By 1640, the missions of San Marcos and San Luis had been established and hence a road all the way to St. Marks and the Tallahassee vicinity must have existed.[7] By 1680, missions and a road had been established all the way to "The Forks", the junction of the Chattahoochee and Flint rivers.[8]

Throughout the years, as the road or roads developed, a variety of names came into use describing the various segments and differing routes of the road. First, one might divide the road into halves. The eastern called in modern terms "The Mission Road", and the western called in the early part of the nineteenth century "Jackson's Trail".

**I. THE MISSION ROAD** extended from Saint Augustine via Mission San Luis to roughly the western tributaries of the Chipola River, which also represented the most westward advance of the Spanish mission system. Its segments and various routes starting from east to west can be named as follows:

A. **THE PICOLATA PATH** (Fig. 12 & 16), so named on Joseph Purcell's 1778 map, extended 138¼ miles from Saint Augustine to the Suwannee River.

B. **THE SAN PEDRO PATHS** (Fig. 16 & 27) can be divided into two routes.
   1. **The San Pedro Path**, again named on Purcell's map, extended 44½ miles from the Suwannee to the Aucilla River. Also, there was an alternate
   2. **Upper San Pedro Path** that forked off the Main San Pedro Path and after 31¼ miles rejoined the Main Path at the Aucilla River. This upper path may not have been considered part of El Camino Real network.

C. **THE APALACHEE PATHS** extended from the Aucilla to the Ochlochnee River and beyond into Georgia. The name "Apalachee Path" is a modern term indicating the route through the territory of the Apalachee Indians, which roughly spanned the lands between the Aucilla and Ochlochnee. There were two main routes that could be taken.
   1. **The Center Path** was perhaps the original route. Its name has been taken from the early American soldiers who accompanied General Andrew Jackson on his march in 1818 through Florida. This path actually forked off the San Pedro Path, but mostly was in Apalachee lands.
   2. **The Old Field Path** (Fig. 27) was Purcell's route and was probably the one described by the soldiers mentioned above as "The Upper Path". It was 63¼ miles long and perhaps reflects an alteration in the path that took place in the eighteenth century as settlement patterns shifted slightly northwards to the Miccosukee settlements. A northwestward extension led to the Chattahoochee River via Burgess (Bainbridge, Georgia). There was also
   3. **The Harmonia (Iamonia?) Path** (Fig. 27) that forked northwestwards off the Old Field Path and after 41 miles rejoined it. It, like the Upper San Pedro Path, may not have been part of El Camino Real network.

---

5. Kevin Hooper, *Early History of Clay County: A Wilderness that could be tamed* (Charleston: The History Press, 2006), 34.

6. John M. Carmody, *The Spanish Missions of Florida* (Washington: Administrative Federal Works Agency, 1940), 35.

7. Carmody, *Spanish Missions of Florida*, 42-43.

8. Verne E. Chatelain, *The Defense of Spanish Florida 1565-1763* (Washington: Carnegie Institution of Washington, Publication 611, 1941), 26.

D. **THE ROAD TO SABACOLA** forked off the Old Field Path between the Ochlochnee and Little rivers, and was the main route beyond the Apalachee lands in the seventeenth century mission period. The Spaniard Diego Pena in 1716 used the above term to describe the road to the Mission Santa Cruz de Sabacola, located at "The Forks" of the Flint and Chattahoochee rivers.

E. **THE ROAD TO CALISTOBLE** continued the above path to the spring Calistoble (Blue Springs in Jackson County).[9] This road serviced the Christianized Chacato (Chatot) Indians, whose lands extended west beyond the Chipola River. A northwestward extension merged with the Red Ground Path at Holmes Creek. Part of this path from Calistoble west should actually fall in the next half of the Spanish Road, namely "Jackson's Trail".

(Left) Figure 5. The Long Road: "It's a long road and sunny, It's a long road and old, And the brown padres made it, For the flocks of the fold."
Frank S. Jones, *History of Decatur County, Georgia*

9. Mark F. Boyd, "Expedition of Marcus Delgado, 1686", *Florida Historical Quarterly* 16, no. 1 (July 1937): 22.

**II JACKSON'S TRAIL** extended from Calistoble or Blue Springs westward to the mouth of the Escambia River, above Pensacola. Besides the western portion of The Road to Calistoble, there were two other segments of Jackson's Trail:

  A. **THE RED GROUND PATH** (Fig. 32 & 40) was 106¼ miles long and was so named for the Red Ground Indian tribe. Their main village in the eighteenth century was Ekanachattee (present Neal's Landing) on the Chattahoochee River. The portion of the trail from the village to Holmes Creek may reflect the eighteenth century northern shift in Indian settlement patterns. This path continued west along the present Alabama/Florida border until it intersected the next segment northwest of Lake Jackson.

  B. **THE LOWER CREEK TRADING PATH** (Fig. 40) was the ancient route from Escambia Bay to the Alabama homeland of the Lower Creeks. While this was essentially a north to south path, its first 79¾ miles were utilized by travelers on the east to west Spanish Road to get from Pensacola to the more northern highlands before proceeding east.

While some scholars may disagree with the names assigned to the varying road segments above, it is acknowledged that all are not contemporaneous with each other, some even being twentieth century designations. The two nineteenth century names "Upper" and "Center" paths imply a "Lower Path". Such a path must have existed at least in the early nineteenth century, but doesn't seem to have been incorporated in the Mission Road network.

# Authors Notes

*On the 500th anniversary of the Spanish discovery of Florida, I have been on a pilgrimage of sorts. I have spent April 5th and 6th searching for the Old Spanish Road, the El Camino Real. I have walked in the footsteps of the Franciscan Fathers (Fig. 6) and the Spanish conquistadors – one group on a peaceful mission to Christianize the Indians; the other on a march to quell a rebellion or repel an invasion from the north.*

*With the use of an 8 ½ foot wide map of 1778 by Joseph Purcell (the only definitive map of the trail), early and present aerial photographs, early U. S. surveys, topographical maps, and an onsite inspection of the evidence, I have plotted the probable route of the most famous road in Florida's history. (Bob Hurst, April 2013)*

Actually, there were many more "pilgrimages" across Florida, but that one in April was one of the most enjoyable, if not the most rewarding. I walked in the footprint of the Old Bellamy Road in historic Newnansville. In Alachua County, I viewed a portion of the Old Spanish Road that became my iconic photograph for the project (Fig. 5). I hiked in the footsteps of ancient travelers as they crossed the Natural Bridge of the Santa Fe River. In Suwannee County, I laughed out loud, when, upon stopping on a road that I suspected of being a footprint of the Old Spanish Road, I looked up at the street sign which said "Old Spanish Road" (The locals knew all along that it was the old trail). In Madison County, I discovered what may have been a Spanish causeway. In Leon County, I found the site of the largest Seminole village along the road, and viewed south of there the highest temple mound in Florida. But I am getting ahead of our travel down El Camino Real. Let us begin where it should start.

Figure 6: The Mission Road. "And lo! A light from heaven shown down. And I beheld through the briars, the Mission Road of the Franciscan Friars." Bob Hurst, April 6, 2013, Charles Spring, Suwannee Co.

CHAPTER ONE

# SAINT AUGUSTINE

*"It was impossible to walk even a quarter of a league without coming into contact with swamps and sloughs...with the result that we are marooned."*

Fray Ruiz, 1600, Saint Augustine[10]

Figure 7. The City Gates, St. Augustine ca. 1861-1865. A view looking into town along St. Georges St. Courtesy Library of Congress.

10 *Carmody,* Spanish Missions of Florida, *21.*

In 1565, the Spanish Admiral Pedro Menendez de Aviles founded Saint Augustine. The city has the distinction of being the oldest continuously occupied European settlement in the United States. From the standpoint of defense, the selection of this site may have had its merits. It had a good harbor and it was surrounded by water and swamp land on three sides. Only from the north was it accessible. It is said, however, that Menendez also founded the town to establish a base for conquest and control of what became the southeastern United States. His defensive peninsula then became an obstacle. Any westward expansion was hindered almost immediately by seemingly impenetrable wet lands, known as the Eastern Valley, but perhaps better defined as the St. John's River Valley

This was only the beginning of the obstacles that the Spaniards encountered with any westward movement. Almost every river and creek across northern Florida flowed from north to south. Every one of these waterways impeded travel across these lands. Compared

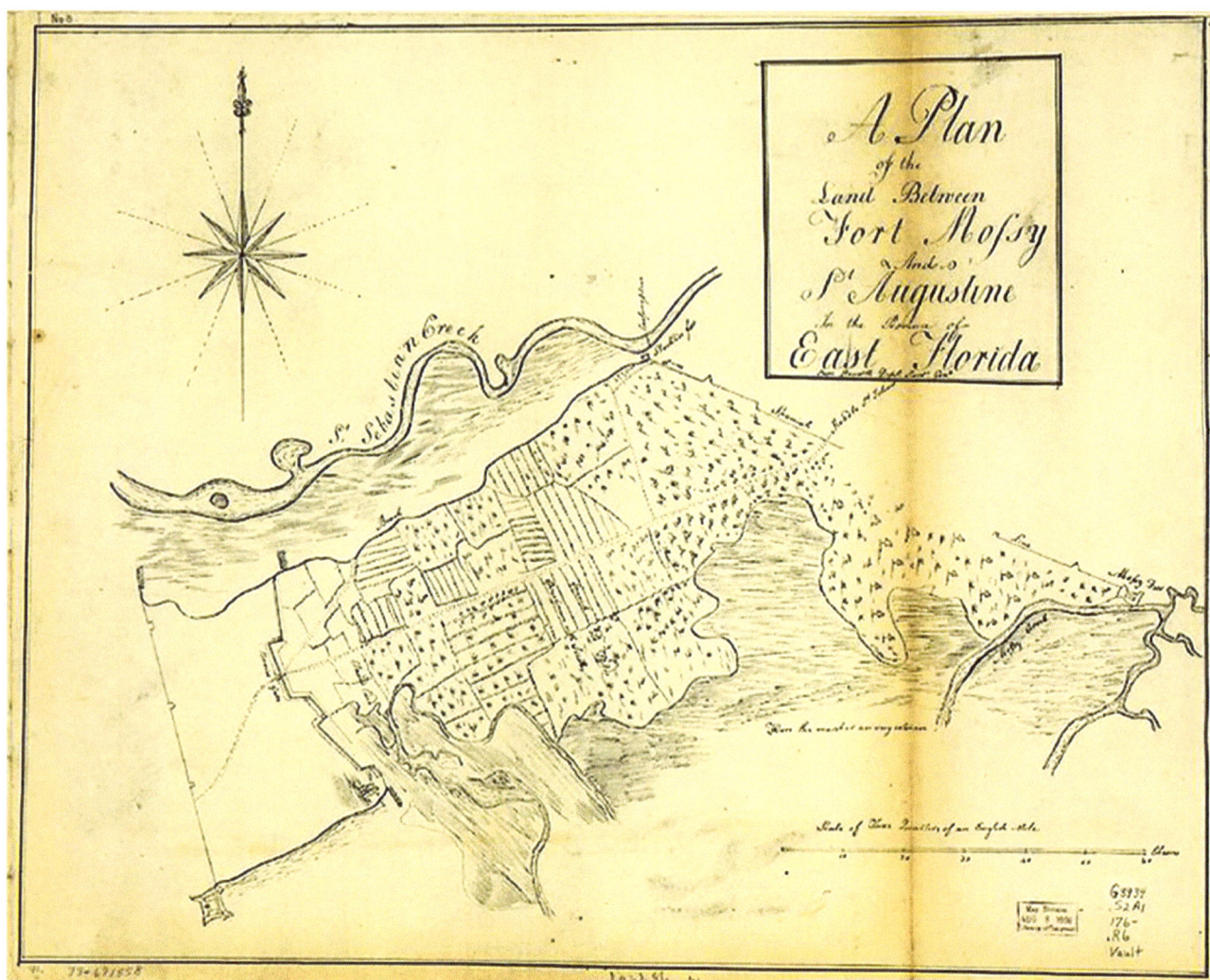

Figure 8: Sam Rosworth's plan of St. Augustine's northern defense, 1765-1775, showing, from left to right, the inner defense or Cubo line, the middle defense or Hornworks with "Barrier Gate", the outer defense or "Spanish Line" with "Stockade Fort", nearby "Crossing Place", and "Mosey Fort". The Picolata Path is shown between the inner and middle defense lines and near the Stockade Fort. Rosworth was the British Surveyor General of Florida. Courtesy Library of Congress, Geography and Map Division..

to this, any incursions from the north into Florida were relatively easy. This was one of the reasons the British and Creek Indians in Georgia and Carolina were able to so successfully invade and destroy the Florida Indian villages and Spanish missions.

CHAPTER TWO

# THE PICOLATA PATH

*"I left the presidio of the said San Augustine,
and camped at the place they call El Pajon, two leagues distant."*

Diego Pena, August 4, 1716[11]

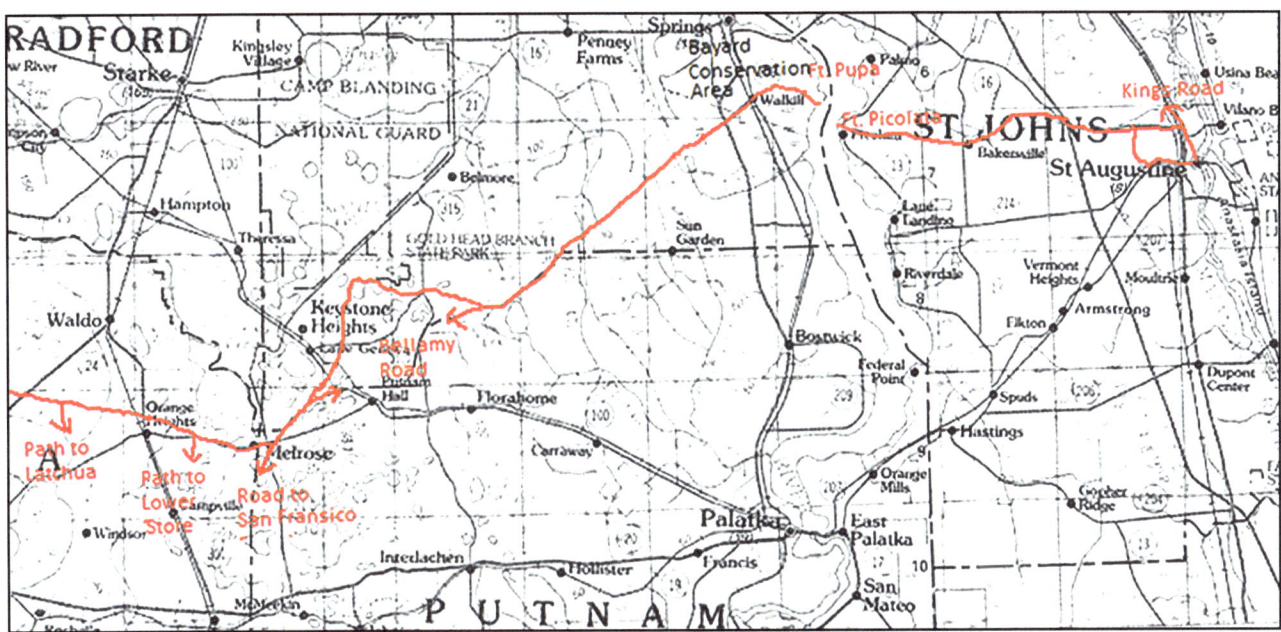

Lieutenant Diego Pena with a small band of soldiers and Indians set out for the provinces of Apalachee and Apalachicola in the year 1716. They rode out of the City Gates (Fig. 7) heading north along the central sand ridge. This ridge road was the way to Georgia (Fig. 8). It was improved during the British period (1764-1783) and became known as the King's Road. They passed through the recently constructed earthworks, known as the "Hornwork". This 15 foot high secondary line of defense was topped with Spanish bayonet plants, and later in the British period, an outer moat was added. They hugged the east bank of the marshy St. Sebastian River until a causeway and bridge allowed them to turn west onto the Camino de Picolata, the Picolata Path. The sand ridge was only the beginning of a series of earlier formed sand dune ridges that the traveler rode up and down as he moved west. The dips between the ridges were marsh and had names such as Fourmile, Fivemile, and Sixmile Swamp, names that indicated the approximate distance along the road from Saint Augustine.

---

11 Mark F. Boyd, "Diego Pena's Expedition to Apalachee and Apalachicola in 1716", *Florida Historical Quarterly* 28, no. 1 (July 1949): 13.

> *"Between Fort Picolata, on the east side of St. John's River, and St. Augustine, the path is chiefly throe low pine lands, part of which is wet and boggy after great rains, [and] is plain and well trod."*
>
> Joseph Purcell, 1778[12]

Pena's party camped at El Pajon, only two leagues (about 5 miles) from Saint Augustine. This was probably the hammock, today called Glimpse of Glory, along present Picolata Road. It was customary for traveling parties to leave late and camp after the first day's march in close proximity to the point of departure, just in case a return was necessary for forgotten equipment and supplies.

The second day they marched across streams and swamps (Fig. 9), skirting the south side of Sixmile Creek ("De La Bria"?). Just to the north of the creek, the American naturalist William Bartram purchased land which later became a plantation known as "Cypress Grove". Going further west, and not far from Picolata, is the site of a Second Seminole War Cemetery (Fig. 10)

Fort Picolata on the east side and Fort Pupa on the west at Bayard Point were established around 1714 by the Spanish to guard the St. Johns River and defend Saint Augustine's western flank. They were made of wood, and were constantly in need of repair.

(Top) Figure 9. Primitive road north of present Picolata Road, St. Johns Co.

(Bottom) Figure 10. Second Seminole War Cemetery, Picolata.

---

12 Boyd, "Map of the Road from Pensacola to St. Augustine", 20.

*" ... at about eight [leagues] from the city of San Agustin ... on each side of the river [St. Johns] ... [is] a sentry box built of boards, eight feet in diameter, named respectively Pupe [San Francisco de Pupa] and Picolata ... both of them [were] surrounded by a palisade, very small and light ... They were ready to crumble down owing to the supports being completely rotten, at the lower part ... [Each was] garrisoned by a squad of eight men, hardly large enough to hold them ... [who have] two swivel guns ... used to protect the couriers and the messengers who go and come from Apalache by land, ... which they cross the river ... on pirogues, as they are often harassed by the Indians while in the act of crossing."*

Antonio de Arredondo, January 22, 1737[13]

Figure 11: "On each side of the river…[is] a sentry box…, named respectively Pupe and Picolata…" St. Johns River looking south with Picolata on the distant left shore and Pupa and Bayard Point on the near right shore. Courtesy Florida History Online, University of North Florida.

13. Hooper, Early History of Clay County, 64

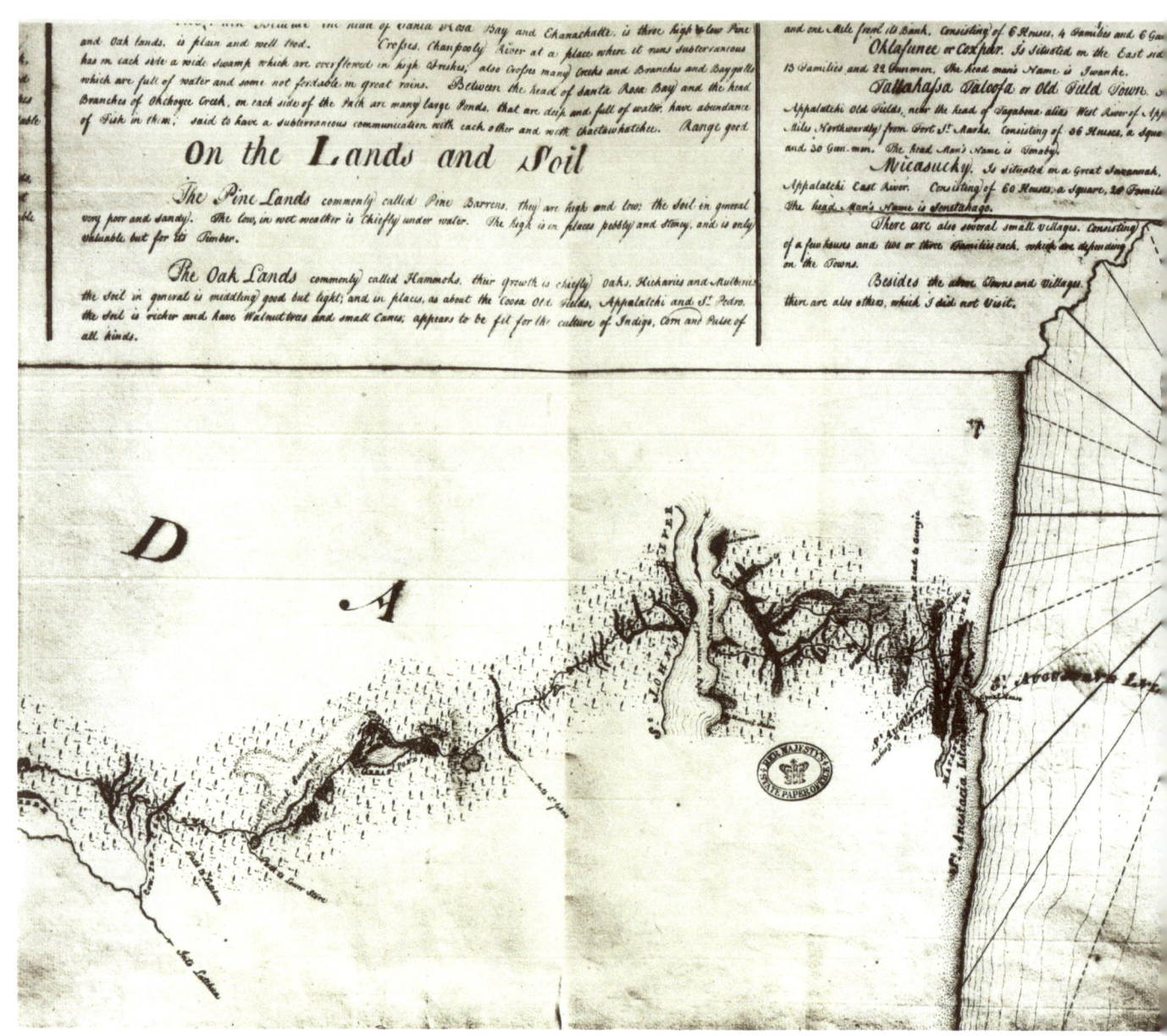

Figure 12: Portion of Joseph Purcell's 1778 Map of the Road from Pensacola in West Florida to St. Augustine in East Florida showing the east segment of the Picolata Path from St. Augustine to Monteocha Creek in present Alachua Co. Courtesy National Archives, UK

Travelers reaching the St. Johns River must have been awed by the obstacle in front of them. One and a quarter mile of a vast expanse of water, that looked more like a bay than a river, now faced them (Fig. 11). Little wonder that it took the above travelers two to three days to cross this waterway.

Things got no better once across the St. Johns River (Fig. 13). Over twenty miles of wetland in today's eastern Clay County had to be traversed (Fig. 14). Three days were needed to reach Florida's elevated Trail Ridge at George's Lake ("Toaputare"), where they camped. Pena encountered six to seven creeks during this time. Three can be identified as Green's (Rio de Blanco), Rice (Ajanoybitta), and Ates (Afanoyvitachirico). All horses contracted "sore mouth" and three Indians became ill.

Travel took its toll on the red man as well as the white man. Supplies for missions had to be hauled overland on the backs of the Indians. Fray Jesus in 1630 reported that because of the distances of 30 to more than 70 leagues, the weight of the burden, the harshness of the terrain, and the miserable condition of the Indians, the cargo bearers arrived "so worn

*"The sixth day was spent awaiting the Indians who were going in my company. They arrived in the afternoon in a canoe. I went in search of another, so that the horses could be taken quickly across, but could not find one. This day the baggage was ferried to the other side of the river [St. Johns], and I camped in Pupa on the [west] bank of the said river. On the seventh day, due to lack of other transport, I was occupied in ferrying the beasts in a canoe."*

Pena, August 6-7, 1716[14]

*"Came to Picolata, and there found all the Indians detained for want of a boat to cross the river [St. Johns]. I immediately sent off a party of soldiers and four white men of my own company to Mr. Godfreys for his flat [boat] ... In the afternoon [of the next day] the party returned with the flat. [The next day] got all the horses over the river."*

Captn. David Holmes, August 9-11, 1778[15]

Figure 13: Bayard Road on the east side of the St. Johns River, Clay Co.

out and vexed" that they were no longer fit for regular work and that some even died from the ordeal. Many of the friars, moved by the suffering of these "sons in Christ", refused to send for provisions allotted them. As a result, the friars, like the Indians, lost their health and became unfit for their tasks.

Not only the Franciscans, but other white men suffered the rigors of travel. In 1595, Governor Avendano made a trip from Saint Augustine to establish missions three to four leagues apart, but the trip proved too rigorous for him, resulting in his death. In 1688, Captain Enrique Primo de Rivera set out from St. Augustine along the road with a cart full of missionary and food stuffs, but had to turn around after only proceeding 80 miles because of impossible streams and swamps. Also in the 1680's, Captain Rivera obtained

14. Boyd, "Diego Pena's Expedition to Apalachee and Apalachicola", 13.

15 Frank S. Jones, History of Decatur County, Georgia, (Spartanburg, SC: The Reprint Co., 1980), 73.

a contract for hauling supplies along the trail as well as maintaining the road. Although he succeeded in maintaining the road in the west, because he failed to do the same in the east, the governor suspended the contract. No, the road was not what one envisions a royal road as being.

This 20 plus mile trek across these wetlands later became known as the Bellamy Road (Fig. 15). Named after its contractor, John Bellamy, this part of the Military or Federal Road was constructed in 1824 to improve and shorten the distance between Saint Augustine and Pensacola. This first American road in Florida precipitated the demise of the Old Spanish Road. While, at least in the east, it was supposed to follow "as near as practical" the old road, John Bellamy took license to alter with shortcuts as he deemed fit. This was very apparent in Clay, Alachua, Madison, Jefferson and Leon counties.

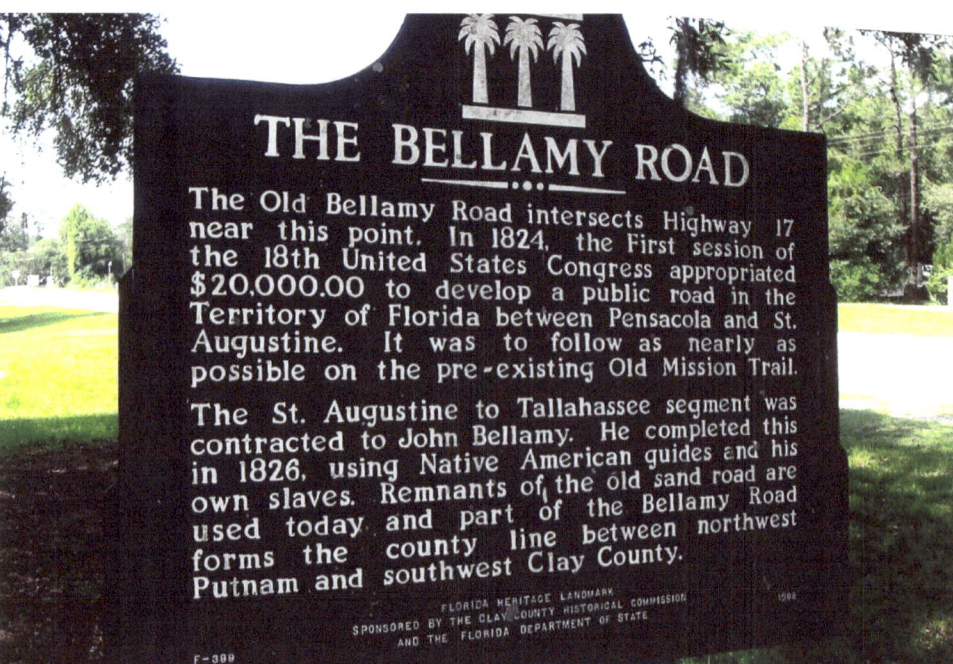

(Top) Figure 14: A muddy Bellamy Road, Clay Co.

(Bottom) Figure 15: Bellamy Road Historic Marker On Us Hwy 17, Clay County

*"Between Santa Fe and St. John's rivers on each side of the path are many large deep ponds full of water in which are abundance of fish; said to have a communication with each other and with the great Latchua pond."*

Joseph Purcell, 1778[16]

Figure 16: Portion of Joseph Purcell's 1778 *Map of the Road from Pensacola in West Florida to St. Augustine in East Florida* showing the western segment of the Picolata Path and the San Pedro Path, or specifically from Monteocha Creek to the Aucilla River. Courtesy National Archives, UK

16 Jerald T. Milanich & Charles Hudson, Hernando de Soto and the Indians of Florida (Gainesville: Univ. Press of Florida, 1993), Figure 44.

The British cartographer must have been referring to the Pleistocene sand dune lakes that are encountered in the present western half of Clay County. From Georges Lake, the road took the traveler up on the prehistoric beachhead and highlands, and on the north side of Hall, Smith, Gator Bone, and White Sands lakes. Purcell mistook this group of four lakes to be one and designated the name "Great Pond" on his map. Bellamy built his road on the south side of this conglomerate of lakes, perhaps along a spur trail to the Spanish mission of Santa Rosa de Ivitanayo, which was on the south side of Hall Lake. Pena refers

to one or perhaps all of these lakes as "Pepayvitta". A Second Seminole War map named this group of lakes "Itoniah Scrub" and labeled the road around the north shore as "Horse Trail" (Fig. 17)[17]. James Goldsborough Bruff labelled them the "Itoniah [Etoniah] Ponds" on his 1846 map entitled "The State of Florida". The Bellamy Road rejoins the Camino Real to the west of Swan Lake.

Pena's group now descended out of the highlands toward the "Latchua", "the sink". He camped at the intersection of the "Road to San Francisco", which approximates State Road 21. Pena had now entered another wetland, today's eastern Alachua County.

Rounding the south shore of Santa Fe Lake, a traveler in Purcell's time of 1778 would have encountered a trail branching off to the south, labelled on his map "Path to lower store". This path appears to approximate NE 211 Drive.

As for the earlier party of Pena, they became lost.

*"I left the said Amaca [a large lake], and without a road set out for a hammock near the town of Santa Fe. This day we marched four leagues, because we knew we were lost."*

Pena, August 15, 1716, somewhere in present Alachua County[18]

Despite Pena's apparent wanderings off trail, evidence from early American surveys and the Purcell map detail a path through the "sink" (eastern Alachua County), paralleling and about two miles north of Hatchet Creek (Purcell's "Pogee Creek"). Just before the creek, the trail is intersected by a "Path to Latchua" (the Alachua Trail, present N. E. 127th Street), according to Purcell. "La Chua" was a Spanish land grant and hacienda owned by the cattle rancher, Captain Thomas Menendez Marquez.

Beyond Hatchet Creek and just before Lake Monteocha Creek, Bellamy once again chose a diversion off the old road. Perhaps he wished to service the settlement of Dell's, which grew into the town of Newnansville, northeast of the present town of Alachua.

The Spanish Road now took a more northwesterly course. About three and a half miles after crossing Rocky Creek, the road now entered higher land. A traveler now found himself travelling through moss covered oaks, perhaps the most beautiful portion of the whole trail. About one mile north of Newnansville and just before crossing Mill Creek, the Spanish Road rejoins the Bellamy Road, but Bellamy successfully straightened the road so that the old more serpentine trace weaves off and again onto the newer road all the way to the Natural Bridge of the Santa Fe River. After crossing the next stream (Townsend Branch), the old road merged with another "Path to Latchua", aka the Florida Santa Fe Trail (Fig. 18). This is where perhaps Hernando De Soto's army, coming from the south, may have merged onto a Pre-Mission Road in 1539 at the Timucuan village of Malapaz.[19]

Figure 17: A Second Seminole War Map showing "Horse Trail" around the "Itoniah Scrub". Courtesy Library of Congress

17 Jerald T. Milanich & Charles Hudson, Hernando de Soto and the Indians of Florida (Gainesville: Univ. Press of Florida, 1993), Figure 44.

18 Boyd, "Diego Pena's Expedition to Apalachee and Apalachicolo", 14.

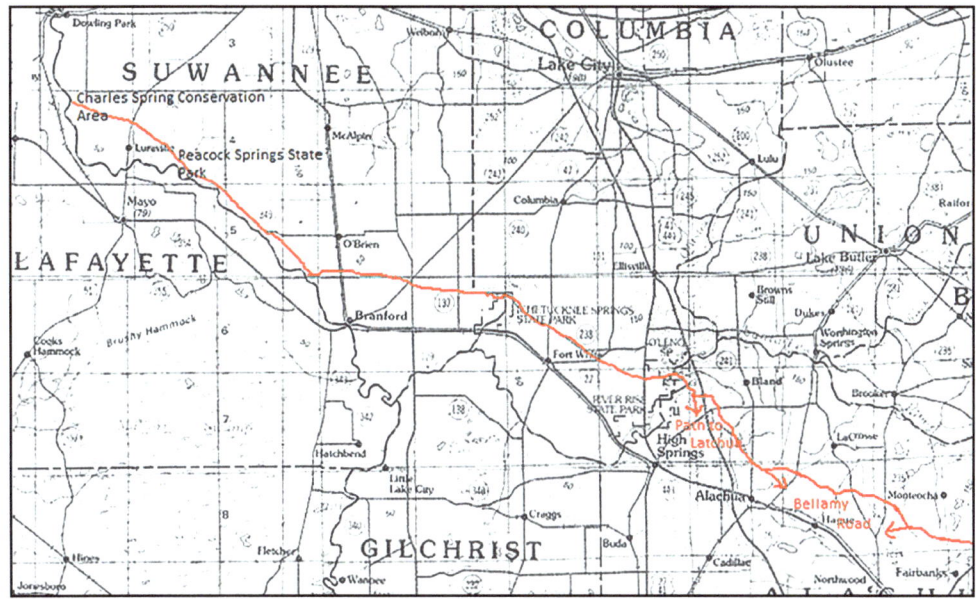

This attests to the belief that the old road followed earlier Indian paths. The so-called De Soto Trail and the Mission Road may now have become one and the same, or, if not the same, closely paralleled all the way to the Ichetucknee River.

By now, the party led by Pena had rejoined the trail and subsequently made camp at the "Rio de Santa Fe". Perhaps his campsite was at "Hekopockee, a noted Indian camping place", according to Purcell. Here the later Alligator and Bellamy roads split and offer two crossings of the Natural Bridge. The Spanish Road followed the Alligator Road into present Oleno State Park, which has a lovely hiking trail called "Paraner's Trail" (Fig. 19 & 20). This trail preserves and mirrors the original road more than any other section in

(Bottom) Figure 18: Private drive off Bellamy Road that may be in the footprint of the old Spanish Road, Alachua Co.

19 *For a thorough discussion of the relation of the Mission Road with the De Soto Trail, see Milanich & Hudson,* Hernando de Soto and the Indians of Florida, *142-154. Milanich and Hudson called the place where the De Soto Trail and the Mission Road merged an "intersection". They incorrectly assumed that the Bellamy Road beyond this point was in fact the Mission Road. The old road at this point took a northerly direction, as did the De Soto Trail, for about a mile, following a ridge, before turning to the northwest.*

Florida.

West of the Santa Fe, the old road roughly followed Bellamy, then present Elim Church Road to Ichetucknee Springs. Here at one of the springs, called Mission or Fig, was located the Spanish mission of San Martin de Timucua or San Martin de Ayaocuto. Remarkable yes and beautiful too. The springs encountered by the traveler in present Columbia and Suwannee counties are too numerous to fully list.

*"Betwixt Seguana [Suwannee] and St. John's rivers, the Path is throe high and low pine lands, the spring Weechatookamee [Ichetucknee] and Santa Fe Old Fields, is plain and well trod ... Betwixt Seguana and Santa Fe on each side of the path are many remarkable rocky springs from 20 to 30 feet deep, said to run subterraneous into the rivers."*

Purcell, 1778[20]

(Top) Figure 19: Paraner's Trail, Oleno State Park.

(Bottom) Figure 20: "The deep indentations in the soil will preserve the road visible for centuries." Dogwood Trail, Oleno State Park

20 *Boyd*, "Diego Pena's Expedition to Apalachee and Apalachicola", 15.

*"The 21st day I left the said site [at Ichetucknee Springs] and camped at a place they call Aquilachua. In this day's march, no creeks were encountered, but there are good springs of water, the first [is] named Usichua, the other Usiparachua, and the other Afanochua."*

Pena, August 21, 1716[21]

The springs encountered on his march from Ichetucknee to the Suwannee River cannot be identified except for Aquilachua. This was probably the sixteenth century Utina Indian village of Aguacalyquen, located near Little River Springs. Here also may have been the seventeenth century Spanish mission of Santa Cruz de Tarihica II. Here the traveler encountered for the first time the "San Juan River", which has been corrupted into the "Suwannee River."

*"In the 22nd I left the said place [Aquilachua] to camp at the first ycapacha [village] of San Juan de Guacara. In this ycapacha are good springs of water. From Calacala [Royal Springs?] which is on the bank of the Rio de Guacara [Suwannee River], one travels in sight of the river as far as Chitonavajuno [Peacock-Baptizing Springs group?]. This Chitonavajuno is a spring of water which has connection with another spring of water."*

Pena, August 22, 1716[22]

Figure 21: "Betwixt Seguana [Suwannee] and Santa Fe on each side of the path are many remarkable rocky springs..." Baptizing Spring, Wes Skiles Peacock Springs State Park, Suwannee Co.

21 Boyd, "Diego Pena's Expedition to Apalachee and Apalachicolo", 15.

22 Ibid.

Other springs along this segment of road are Running and Cow Springs. At Baptizing Springs was the seventeenth century Spanish mission of San Juan de Guacara (Fig. 21).

From the springs, Pena's group left the Suwannee, marching northwest to once again encounter the river at Charles Spring, the location of the 2nd Spanish Mission San Juan de Guacara (Fig. 22). The spring was the ancient crossing of the river. This was the first major river crossing that the traveler faced since the broad St. Johns River. Reuben Charles and family established a ferry and trading post here in 1824.

Figure 22: Charles Spring, Suwannee Co.

## CHAPTER THREE

# THE SAN PEDRO PATH

*"I camped on the [other side of the] Rio de San Juan de Guacara ... (Suwannee River) [The next day] I remained at this spot in order to rest the animals, which were much fatigued from swimming the river, which although not very wide, now has a strong current. It is about a pistol shot in width. There is much game, deer and buffalo, hereabouts ... All this land is elevated, there are no thick woods, but good watering places. The only drawback is that the roads are obliterated by the fallen timber which has lodged in them."*

Pena, August 24, 1716[23]

Pena was now at present Ezell Landing in Lafayette County (Fig. 23). Another path and adventure now lay ahead.

The term "Old Fields" refers to the fields, cultivated by the Timucua and Apalache Indians and the Spanish, who once occupied these lands.

The early Spanish armies of Panfilo de Narvaez in 1527 and of Hernando De Soto in 1539

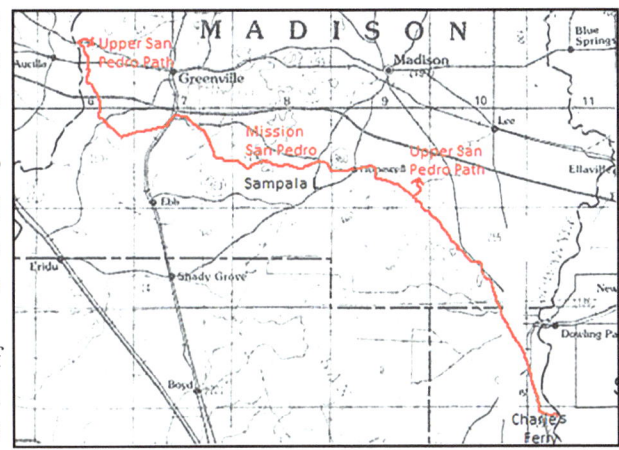

*"Betwixt Micasukey and Seguana [Suwannee] River, the main St. Pedro Path is through oak, high and low pine lands and St. Pedro Old Fields, [and] is plain and well trod."*

Purcell, 1778[24]

probably traveled this route. Later travelers must have been amazed by the ruins that they now passed through, evidence of a once great Spanish Florida and the powerful Timucua and Apalachee nations.

Although travel was still not easy, evidence abounded of Spanish efforts to improve and maintain the old road (Fig. 24). At Mill Creek (Pena's "Usybitta"?) on the present

23 Ibid.

24 Boyd, "A Map of the Road from Pensacola to St. Augustine", 19.

*"The Appalatchi and St. Pedro Old Fields bear the marks of once having been large and flourishing Spanish settlements strongly proved by the ruins of forts, churches, and other buildings; the cannon and church bells that are found lying about; the broad roads; and by the remains of causeways and bridges that are seen to this day."*

Purcell, 1778[25]

(Top) Figure 23: "I camped on the [other side of the] Rio de San Juan de Guacara [Suwannee River]...I remained at this spot in order to rest the animals, which were much fatigued from swimming the river, which although not very wide, now has a strong current. It is about a pistol shot in width." Ezell Landing on the Suwannee River, Lafayette Co.

(Bottom) Figure 24: Old St. Augustine Road, Madison Co.

*25 Boyd, "A Map of the Road from Pensacola to St. Augustine", 21*

Madison-Lafayette county line was a bridge. Passing by "Ococo" (Pine Lake?), two other lakes ("Guihenayoa" and "Ticosoriva"), and the intersection of an alternate route ("Upper St. Pedro Path"), the traveler came to Lake Sampala. Perhaps the lake's name is a corruption of San Pablo.[26] Here was the Yustaga Indian mission of San Pedro y San Pablo de Potohiriba, the largest in this region. In 1778, Purcell noted "St. Pedro Pond" and the "Ruins of St. Pedro Fort". John Bellamy in 1824 chose to diverge from the old road, and build his road south of Sampala Swamp. The Bellamy or Military or Federal Road was to no longer follow the old road. After Potohiriba, Lieutenant Pena chose to fork to the southeast along another branch of the El Camino Real, probably the present Lake Sampala Road. This road merged with Bellamy's, which then continued west to the Aucilla River.

Between here and the Aucilla River were the remains of a Spanish bridge and causeway. Purcell designates the site as "Bridge River and remains of Spanish Bridge and Causeway". There appears to be no river here now, but what Purcell saw may have been a branch of Sundown or Alligator Creek. Near the site is still evidence of an elevated road bed.

The course of the old road had now taken the travelers west along the south edge of Hixtown Swamp. Passing this obstacle, the road turned north northeast, crossing the Little Aucilla River, which is no more than a creek. Purcell's "Upper St. Pedro Path", mentioned above, after going around the north side of the swamp, now merges with the main road. The road now reaches the next major river, the Aucilla.

*26 John H. Hann, A History of the Timucua Indians and Missions (Gainesville: UF Press, 1996), 183.*

CHAPTER FOUR

# THE OLD FIELD PATH

*"Of the head of [the Aucilla River] nothing certain is known. The path from Mikasukey to Sahwanne which crosses it at or near the sources strikes it twenty miles from the first place in a course of about north 48 east. At this present, the creek either rises in or has swelled to a large grassy pond four hundred yards wide and with a strong current in the middle. Its course thence to the crossing of the lower route is nearly south and hence to the mouth extent about eighty miles ... The tract on the Assilla extends seven or eight miles down the creek a little below the CENTER PATH ... Below the LOWER PATH the country is similar to that on New River ... a quarter mile below the LOWER PATH there is a natural bridge over the creek."*

Captain Hugh Young with General Jackson's army, 1818[27]

Captain Young is referring here to the crossings of the Aucilla on the three routes of "The Path", those being the Upper, the Center, and the Lower Path. The Upper Path is the one that Captain Holmes with Purcell travelled. It crossed the Aucilla near the present US 90 crossing. The Center Path is probably the one Bellamy chose to build his road to Tallahassee, the one that Lieutenant Pena took on his march west, and the route that General Jackson chose on his Suwannee River Campaign. It crossed the Aucilla about two miles below the US19/27 crossing.

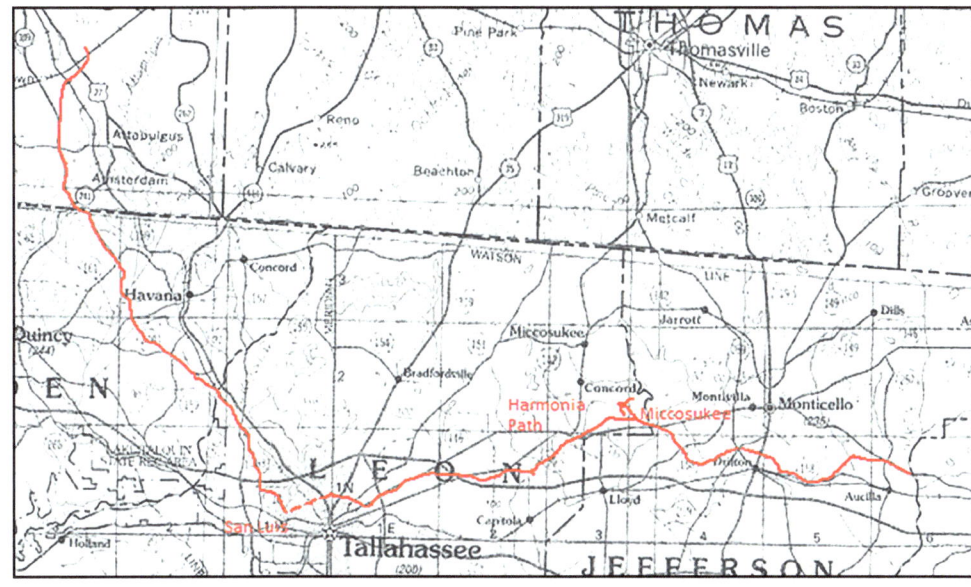

27 Young, "Topographical Memoir on East and West Florida", no. 1 (July 1934), 42-43.

The land ahead once belonged to the Apalachee nation, the most powerful and richest province in the sixteenth and seventeenth centuries. The Upper or Old Field Path (Fig. 27) now closely follows the present Drifton-Aucilla Highway, then northwest to Casa Blanca at the crossroads of the El Camino Real and the Bellamy/Federal Road. Casa Blanca, "the White House", was built in 1827 by Colonel Joseph M. White, Florida's first delegate to Congress.

Beyond there the road skirted the south shore of Lake Miccosukee and now entered present Leon County. Almost immediately, two Native American sites are encountered. About one mile south was the Letchworth-Love Temple Mound complex, where Florida's tallest Indian mound can be seen (Fig. 25). Its builders were the Weeden Island Culture that existed between 200 and 800 A.D.

The second site is the Indian village of Miccosukee.

(Top) Figure 25: The tallest Indian mound in Florida. Letchworth-Love Mounds Archaeological State Park, Jefferson Co.

(Bottom) Figure 26: Sunray Road, possibly atop the Spanish Road near the Miccosukee settlements, Leon Co.

Figure 27: Portion of Joseph Purcell's 1778 *Map of the Road from Pensacola in West Florida to St. Augustine in East Florida,* showing the western segment of the San Pedro Path, the Old Field Path and the east segment of the Road through Georgia, or from Hicks Lake in Madison Co. to Spring Creek near present Brinson, GA. Also shown are the Upper San Pedro and the Harmonia Paths.

"Early this morning Lieut. [Timothy] Barnard, Mr. Burgess [a trader who resided on the site that became present Bainbridge, Georgia] and myself set off for Micasuque, where we arrived in the afternoon. The Indians expected us there, and were all seated in the Square accordingly, and had black drink ready for us which they served up soon after our arrival, with all the usual ceremony."

Holmes, August 7, 1778[28]

"Micasuckey is situated on a great savannah [Lake Miccosuckee], the head of the Appalatchi East River. Consisting of 60 houses, a square, 28 families and 70 gunmen. The head man's name is Senetahago."

Purcell, 1778[29]

---

[28] Jones, History of Decatur County, 67.

[29] Boyd, "A Map of the Road from Pensacola to St. Augustine", 23.

A traveler in the seventeenth century might have encountered Native Americans of the Apalachee Nation; however, after the devastating raids of the British and Creek Indians in 1704, a void was created, which was slowly inhabited by Indian tribes from the north, called Seminoles. One of these tribes were the Miccosukee. Their village, described above, was the largest village that the traveler would have encountered in the eighteenth century (Fig. 26).

Here at the village was a fork in the old road. The main road now led southwest to the Spanish mission of San Pedro de Patale . A northwest path called "the Harmonia [Iamonia?] Path" led around the north side of Lake Iamonia and toward the Flint River crossing in Georgia.

# CHAPTER FIVE

# THE CENTER PATH

As mentioned above Lieutenant Pena after the San Pedro mission chose a path that led southwest toward a line of missions situated on the Florida highlands and close to the Cody Escarpment. Approximately two miles southwest of Lake Sampala, the Spanish Road merges with the later Bellamy Road and then continues west passing a Spanish mission site, perhaps Santa Elena de Machava and the "Hammock of San Pedro" (perhaps the small present community of Ebb). Just before the Aucilla River, there were two other Spanish missions, perhaps San Matheo de Tolanatofi and a second Santa Elena de Machava.

*"I found [the Aucilla River] so swollen that the beasts were obliged to swim the flood. It was very laborious to open a road here. In this river, my horse was drowned, and I narrowly escaped, because in leading it into the river by halter, the current caught us and forced us down on a tree, toppled by the weather, which had fallen in midstream, in the branches of which I could not avoid entanglement."*

Pena, September 2, 1716[30]

While the Aucilla is normally small, it can be a formidable challenge in flood stage. Pena's crossing may have been two to three miles below the present US Highway 27 bridge.

The earlier Hernando De Soto expedition had an equally difficult time crossing the Aucilla.

*"...they [the soldiers] came to a swamp that was very large and difficult*

30  Boyd, "Diego Pena's Expedition to Apalachee and Apalachicolo", 16-17.

> to cross, because the water alone, without the woods that were on either side, was half a league wide and as long as a river. At the edges of the swamp beyond the water was a forest with a great deal of thick and tall timber and much underbrush consisting of blackberry vines and other small growth, which, being interwoven with the large trees, so thickened and closed up the forest that it had the appearance of a stout wall. Therefore, there was no passage for crossing the woods and the swamp except by a path the Indians had made, so narrow that two men abreast could scarcely go along it.
>
> " ... They found that all of it could be forded waist and thigh-deep except in midchannel, where for a distance of forty paces, because of the great depth, it was crossed by a bridge made of two fallen trees and other timbers fastened together. They saw also that under the water was a path just as there was through the woods, clear of brush and vines that were on either side, off the path."

Garcilaso de la Vega writing on the events of October 1, 1539[31]

An elevated finger of land with an east-west axis provided a natural causeway on the west side of the river, where the land is otherwise a marshy flood plain. This raised sliver of land not only provided a roadway but also the site of a mission, probably San Miguel de Asile. Its southern boundary was the Cody Escarpment. De la Vega writing a century and a half earlier described this area as a woodland, but not as thick as the one immediately adjacent the river swamp.[32]

Now in Apalachee territory, Pena visited the Mission San Miguel de Asile near the river, and San Lorenzo de Ivitachuco near Lake Iamonia and Welaunee Creek ["the Creek of Ybitachuco"]. Travel had taken its toll on Pena's group:

> "I remained at [the creek of Ybitachuco], because of the heavy rain, since the clothing already had fallen in pieces from our bodies, as day and night it has been raining excessively upon us, and if there be added wind, mosquitos and ticks, [it] appears imprudent [to prosecute] a similar journey. God help us."

Pena, September 4, 1716[33]

Pena's group traveled west, passing the missions La Conception de Ayubale, San Francisco de Ocone, and San Juan de Aspalaga. For a few miles, the Federal Road utilized a portion of the road and is still called "The Old St. Augustine Road." De la Vega

---

31  Garcilasco de la Vega, Florida of the Inca, www.floridahistory.com/Inca-5.html.

32  Garcilasco de la Vega, The Florida of the Inca, trans. and ed. John Grier Varner & Jeannette Johnson Varner (Austin, U. of Texas Press, 1951), 179-180.

33  Boyd, "Diego Pena's Expedition to Apalachee and Apalachicolo", 17.

described this portion of the land as open, level and free of timber. Probably near Lake Catherine was the beginning of scattered houses and cultivated land with fields of corn, beans, squash and other vegetables on both sides of the road and as far as the eye could see.[34] Approaching the St. Marks River and Mission Capole, Pena encountered more bad weather, perhaps even a tornado spawned by a hurricane.

*"I cannot exaggerate the severity of the weather which we experience to our great confusion. I mention here that which was seen in the chicasa [village] of Capole, which is that the wind broke a pine of moderate size in the middle, and the half of the tree was caught without falling more than four fathoms, making a furrow like that of a plow, a thing incredible even to the Indians. They are thinking that God is aiding us."*

Pena, September 6, 1716[35]

Now turning north and paralleling the St. Marks River on their left, Pena traveled to the headwaters of the river. De la Vega described this trek as lacking cultivation and house, but clear of foliage.[36] It should be noted here that none of the travelers, Pena, Purcell, and even the army of De Soto, mention crossing the St. Marks. The explanation is that they went north and simply went around the river.[37] Near the source of the river, Pena encountered the Mission San Pedro de Patale.

*"This place of Patale is where the Reverend Father fray Manuel de Mendoza sacrificed his life, finishing his life preaching the Holy Evangels. There were also martyrized many Spaniards and Indians by fire, [who] when they screamed were mocked. Four soldiers died as martyrs. God forgive them."*

Pena, September 6, 1716[38]

Pena spoke here of one of the raids carried out by the English and Creeks in the year 1704. This particular raid was evidently without English leadership. Father Mendoza was shot, the convent burned, and many villagers made captive.[39]

It was at Patale that Purcell's northerly Old Field Path rejoined the Center Path that Pena used.

---

34  Vega, *The Florida of the Inca*, 182.

35  Boyd, "Diego Pena's Expedition to Apalachee and Apalachicolo", 17-18.

36  Vega, *The Florida of the Inca*, 183.

37  The trace of this portion of the road can still be seen on early aerial photographs.

38  Boyd, "Diego Pena's Expedition to Apalachee and Apalachicolo", 17.

39  Mark F. Boyd, Hale G. Smith & John W. Griffin, *Here They Once Stood, The Tragic End of the Apalachee Missions* (Gainesville: U. of Florida Press, 1951), 16.

*"Betwixt Tallahassa Taloofa and Micasuky, the path is through Appalatchi Old Fields, pine and oak lands, in places along old broad roads worn one, two and three feet deep, [and] is plain and well trod."*

Purcell, 1778[40]

Along no other portion of the road traveled by Purcell and his entourage does he speak of such a deep and well-traveled part as he does the section from Miccosukee to the Tallahassee area. This is quite evident even today on at least one site along the old trail, close to the intersection of the Wadesboro Road and Mahan Drive (U. S. Highway 90). Despite the difficulty in reconnoitering this site due to the overgrowth, the old roadway cut is approximately five and one half feet deep and 46 feet wide from the edge of its shoulders. The actual road bed is 24 feet wide (Fig. 28).

The old road now continued west along the hilly ridges of today's Leon County and eventually merging with today's Old Miccosukee Road, and then southwest into the Tallahassee area. De la Vega described the surrounding land as of a good quality, fertile with an abundance of food and fish, and interspersed with villages with 50, 60 and even 100 houses. The principle village, Anhaica, was located on a hill a little east of Florida's old capital building, and consisted of 250 houses.[41] Despite the difficulty of tracing the old route through present Tallahassee, the early route probably led down to one of the seven hills of Tallahassee, where the old Capital now stands. From there it led westward to Mission San Luis, which stood on another of the hills of Tallahassee. The reconstructed Mission and Fort today gives the visitor an idea of what mission life was like.

Encountering several mission villages on Pena's trip to San Luis, he saw cattle, especially buffalo, and fruit trees, such as fig, peach, pomegranate, quince, medlar, chestnut, and acorn (oak). Little wonder that the name "Old Field" was applied to this Apalachee region. In fact, the Miccosukee word "Tallahassee" means "old field".

The 18th century route led to the Miccosukee town of Tallahassee Taloofa, also on a hill according to Captain Young. That route probably closely followed present Betton and Bradford roads. The U. S. survey notes of 1824 mark a coordinate close to the Bradford-Meridian Road intersection as "old trace".

---

40  Boyd, "A Map of the Road from Pensacola to St. Augustine", 18.

41  Vega, *The Florida of the Inca*, 184.

(Top) Figure 28: "old broad roads worn one, two and three feet deep...plain and well trod." Deep cut (to left of fence) near US Highway 98 and Wadesboro Road, Tallahassee.

*"Tallahassee Tolofa or Old Field is situated in the Apalatche Old Fields, near the head of Tagabona alias West River of Apalatche [perhaps Munson Slough], about 10 miles northwardly from Fort St. Marks, consisting of 36 houses, a square, 16 families, and 30 gunmen. The head man's name is Tonaby."*

Purcell, 1778[42]

Captain Young with Jackson's army speaks of a degenerative settlement:

*"[Concerning the] Tallehassas. Settled on the road from Okalokina to Mikasukey numbers only fifteen. Chief Okiakhija a weak man and unfriendly. Character worthless, dishonest and inveterately hostile. They have neither arts nor cattle, but their land is excellent and gave them fine crops with very little labour."*

Young, 1818[43]

Beyond San Luis and Tallahassee Talofa, the road took a northwest course (Fig. 29). The present Old Bainbridge Road probably follows the course at least to Lake Jackson, which was referred to as a prairie or savannah by the early travelers.

*"I ... camped at the large prairie of Ocalquibe, which extends for more than a league. On the prairie there was seen more than 300 cattle buffalo and a few cows. Five buffalo, two cows, and eleven deer were killed."*

Pena, September 8, 1716[44]

42  Boyd, "A Map of the Road from Pensacola to St. Augustine", 22-23.

43  Young, "Topographical Memoir on East and West Florida", no. 2, 88.

44  Boyd, "Diego Pena's Expedition to Apalachee and Apalachicolo", 18.

(Left) Figure 29: Old Bainbridge Road, Tallahassee.

Purcell refers to it as the Great Savannah Okaheepee.

Beyond Lake Jackson, the Seaboard Coast Railroad follows the old road across the Ochlocknee River. Early travelers refer to this river by several names. The Spaniard Juan Fernandez de Florencia in his 1677 interview with the Indians on their expedition to lands beyond San Luis called it "River Lagino".[45] The Spaniard Marcos Delgado in his march from Apalachee to the Upper Creek country in 1686 called it "the water" (el agua).[46] Another Spaniard, Torres y Ayala, who travelled from Apalachee to Pensacola, called it the Amarillo River.[47]

The Ochlocknee was an important political boundary. Bishop Gabriel Diaz Vara Calderon described it thusly:

*"At 2 leagues from the afore-mentioned village of San Luis, on the northern frontier, is the river Agna [Ochlocknee] which divides the provinces of Apalache and Apalachicoli ... "*

Bishop Calderon, circa 1676[48]

Pena gave the following account of the river crossing:

*"The crossing of the Rio de Lagna was laborious, as one had to swim a quarter of a league, requiring all of one day for the crossing, since all of the channels were full. For this, a boat was made from a green buffalo hide. The hide with its gunwales, ribs and stem holds three persons, or more than a dozen arrobas of baggage."*

Pena, September 10, 1716[49]

Now in the province of the Apalachicoli natives, the present Shady Rest Road follows the old trail. Ayala stated:

*"We ... finally came to the village of San Cosme and San Damien Yecambi (present community of Scotland?). It is three leagues from San Luis to this place ... "*

Ayala, June 8, 1693[50]

Pena refers to one of these villages as the "Chicaza of Scambe" (Escambe), a possible mission site.[51]

Passing these villages, a traveler faced a fork in the road. The seventeenth century route continued west, while the 18th century road as mapped by Purcell turned northwards.

---

45. John H. Hann, "Apalachee Leader's Report on their 1677 Expedition against the Chisca." Unpublished attachment to a letter, in possession of the writer, July 3, 2001.

46. Boyd, "Expedition of Marcos Delgado, 1686", 22

47. Irving Leonard, "Journal of Don Laurenzo de Torres y Ayala from the Expedition he made overland from San Luis de Apalachee to the Bay of Pensacola in the year of 1693, August 5, 1693" in Spanish Approach to Pensacola, 1689-1693 (Albuquerque: The Quivira Society, 1939), 230.

48. Gabriel Diaz Vara Calderon, "Florida and the Florida Missions", in A 17th Century Letter of Gabriel Diaz Vara Calderon, Bishop of Cuba, Describing the Indians and Indian Missions of Florida, trans. Lucy L. Wenhold (Washington: Smithsonian Institution, Nov. 20, 1936), 7

49. Boyd, "Diego Pena' Expedition to Apalachee and Apalachicolo", 19.

50. Leonard, "Journal of Don Laurenzo de Torres y Ayala", 230.

51. Boyd, "Diego Pena's Expedition to Apalachee and Apalachicolo", 19.

CHAPTER SIX

# THE ROAD THROUGH GEORGIA

*"Betwixt Ekanachatte and Tallahassa Taloofa, the Path is through high pine and oak lands and the Appalatchi Old Field, [and] is plain and well trod in places along old carriage roads worn one and two feet deep."*

Purcell, 1778[52]

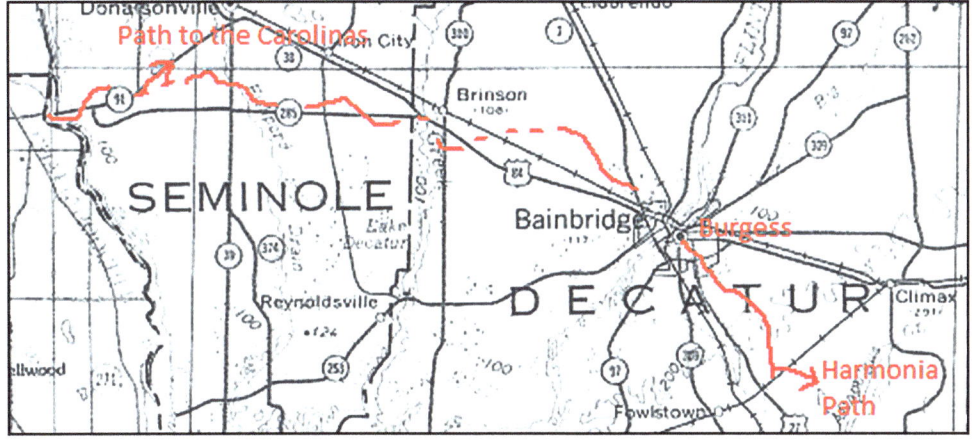

Purcell in referring to "carriage roads" probably simply meant "transport road", rather than a road bearing the marks of a wheeled carriage.

After leaving the earlier road, now the Shady Rest Road, the 18th century road crossed Hurricane Creek, then Attapulgus Creek before the stream merges with Willacoochee Creek to form Little River. Present Dogtown and Salem Roads, and then Georgia's Fowlstown Road probably follow its path along a watershed ridge between Willacoochee and Attapulgus creeks north northwestwards. Finally, able to pass the headwaters of Little Attapulgus Creek, the old road turned north northeastwards, then north northwestwards (Fig. 30) approaching Burgess (present Bainbridge) on what is now the Lake Douglas Road. James Burgess, the earliest white settler in the area that became Bainbridge, was a trader, who provided lodging and aid to Captain David Holmes and Purcell.

Crossing the Flint River near the Seaboard Coast Railroad bridge, the road continued west northwestwards to "the Springs" (Spring Creek). With few geographic features, this trek would have been fairly uneventful for the traveler. Today it is farmed and probably most traces of the old road have been erased by the plow (Fig. 31).

52. Boyd, "A Map of the Road from Pensacola to St. Augustine", 18

53. Jones, History of Decatur County, 62

(Top) Figure 30: "...along old carriage roads worn one and two feet deep." Toole Dairy Road off Lake Douglas Road, Bainbridge.

(Bottom) Figure 31: Primitive road off Zorn Road, perhaps one of the few remains of the road in Georgia, West Bainbridge.

*"This morning we set off and arrived at the Springs, which we crossed with all our baggage in a leather canoe."*

Holmes, August 2, 1778[53]

The crossing of Spring Creek was probably less than a quarter of a mile north of the present US 84 bridge, near the abandoned lumber mill at Brinson, Georgia. The old two rut road out of Brinson to the creek may be in the footprint of the El Camino Real.

The road from the Springs to the Chattahoochee River passed Rock Pond. Sections of two old roads may preserve part of the road. A section of the old Donalsonville Road from the community of Lela to Fishpond Drain may preserve the road. Also, the old road from Neal's Landing to Steam Mill may lie in its footprint. Just before reaching the Chattahoochee, the road may have merged with an even older trading path that led northeast into Georgia and the Carolinas.

The crossing of the Chattahoochee River was just to the south of the present State Road 2, where the Seminole village of "Ekanachattee" or "Red Ground" (present Neal's Landing) was located.

*"This day we arrived at an Indian Town called Ekanachatee consisting of about twenty two Gun Men. It being the time of their Busk I was obliged to defer making them acquainted with my business until the Ceremony was over. In the meantime they received us with great friendship and showed us every mark of distinction that we could expect."*

Holmes, July 25, 1778[54]

*"Ekanachatte or Red Ground is situated on the West Bank of Chattahutchee River, consisting of 26 houses, a chuko-thlacko or great house, commonly called a square; 10 families and 10 gunmen. The head man or chief is named Cockee, commonly called by the traders, 'the Bully'."*

Purcell, 1778[55]

Archaeological excavations at Neals Landing in 1987 for the U. S. Army Corps of Engineers plus archival evidence indicated the site was probably the Creek village of Ekanachattee.[56]

Purcell describes a spur trail leading southwest from Ekanachattee, called "The Trading Path from the Head of Santa Rosa Bay to Ekanachattee" (Fig. 32). This one hundred mile path was considered a short cut to Pensacola. It crossed the Natural Bridge of the Chipola above Marianna, and terminated at a trading post at the mouth of the Choctawhatchee River. Captain Holmes and Purcell took this route to Pensacola on their return march from St. Augustine. The last portion of their journey had to be done by boat.

From Ekanachattee westwards and into Alabama was the Red Ground Path. Before proceeding along this path, a description of the seventeenth century path from Little River westwards should be made.

This path continued along the route of the present Shady Rest Road (State Road 270) to Little River. The Spaniards Delgado, Ayala and Pena, in that order, all travelled this route

---

54. Ibid.

55. Boyd, "A Map of the Road from Pensacola to St. Augustine", 22.

56. "National Register Testing at Neals Landing", www.earth-search.com/NEALS.htm.

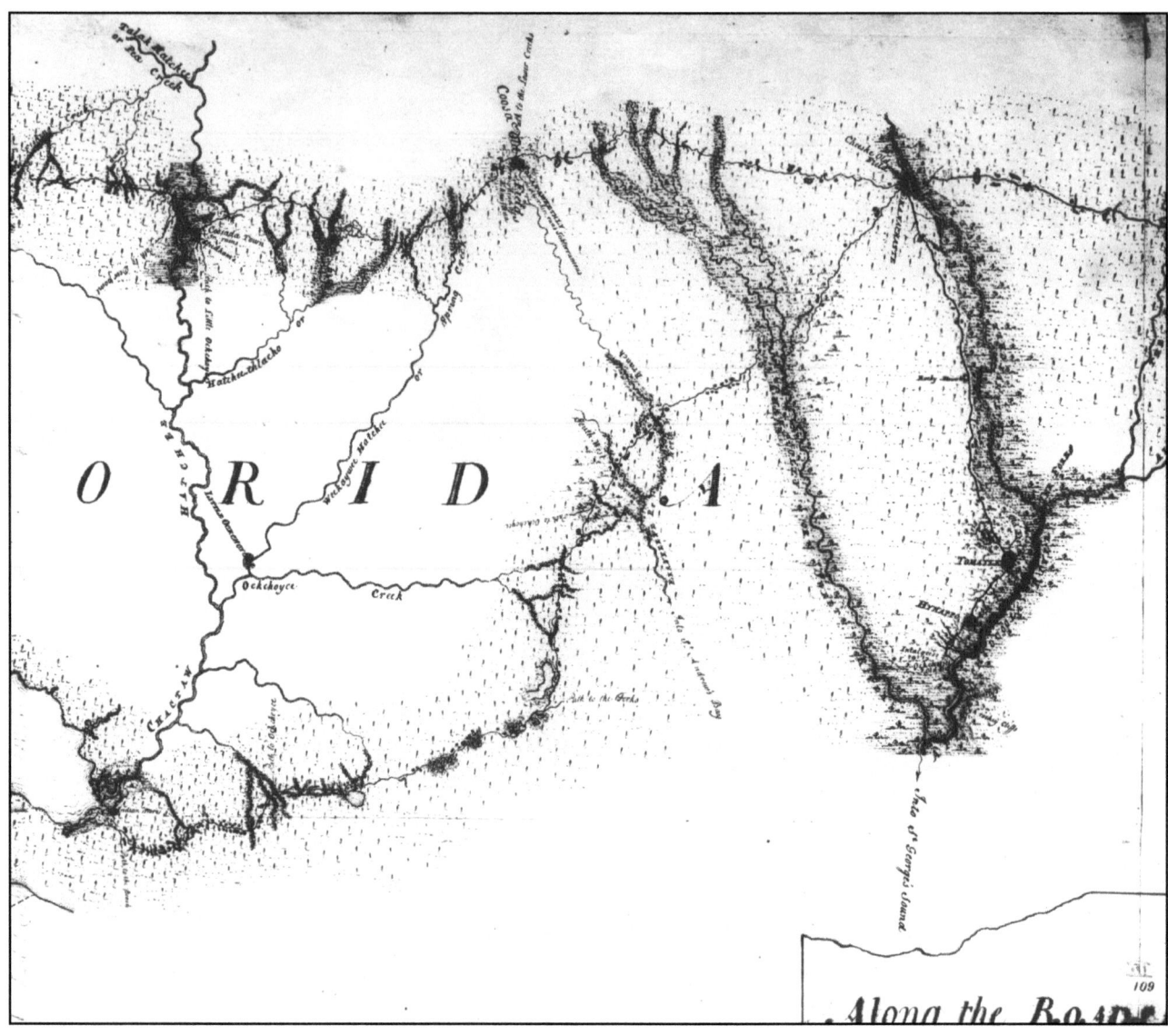

Figure 32: Portion of Joseph Purcell's 1778 *Map of the Road from Pensacola in West Florida to St. Augustine in East Florida* showing the west segment of the Road through Georgia and east segment of Red Ground Path, or Spring Creek near Brinson, GA to Limestone Creek in Walton Co. Courtesy National Archives, UK.

## CHAPTER SEVEN

# THE ROAD TO SABACOLA

*"This day marched four leagues, crossing the Rio de Palos [Little River], which has much hammock on both sides. The river is more or less a stone throw in width. A raft of logs was made [for crossing]. Here were killed a bull, two cows and a large deer ...*
*This route is the old road to Savacola [Sabacola]. "*

Pena, September 11, 1716[57]

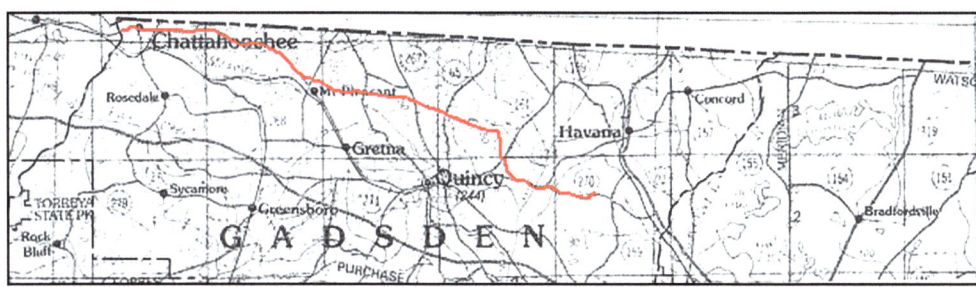

(Below) Figure 33: Segment of Vincente Sebastian Pintado's *Plano Borrador del limite comun a las dos Floridas y de los territories de ambas provincias adyacentes e el,* ca. 1815. Courtesy Library of Congress.

Perhaps the early map done by the Spanish Surveyor General of West Florida, Vincente Sebastian Pintado (Fig. 33), gave a hint as to the route once across Little River.[58] "Senda de Thomson a Apalache" is shown taking a northwest course near the present community

57. Boyd, "Diego Pena's Expedition to Apalachee and Apalachicolo", 19.

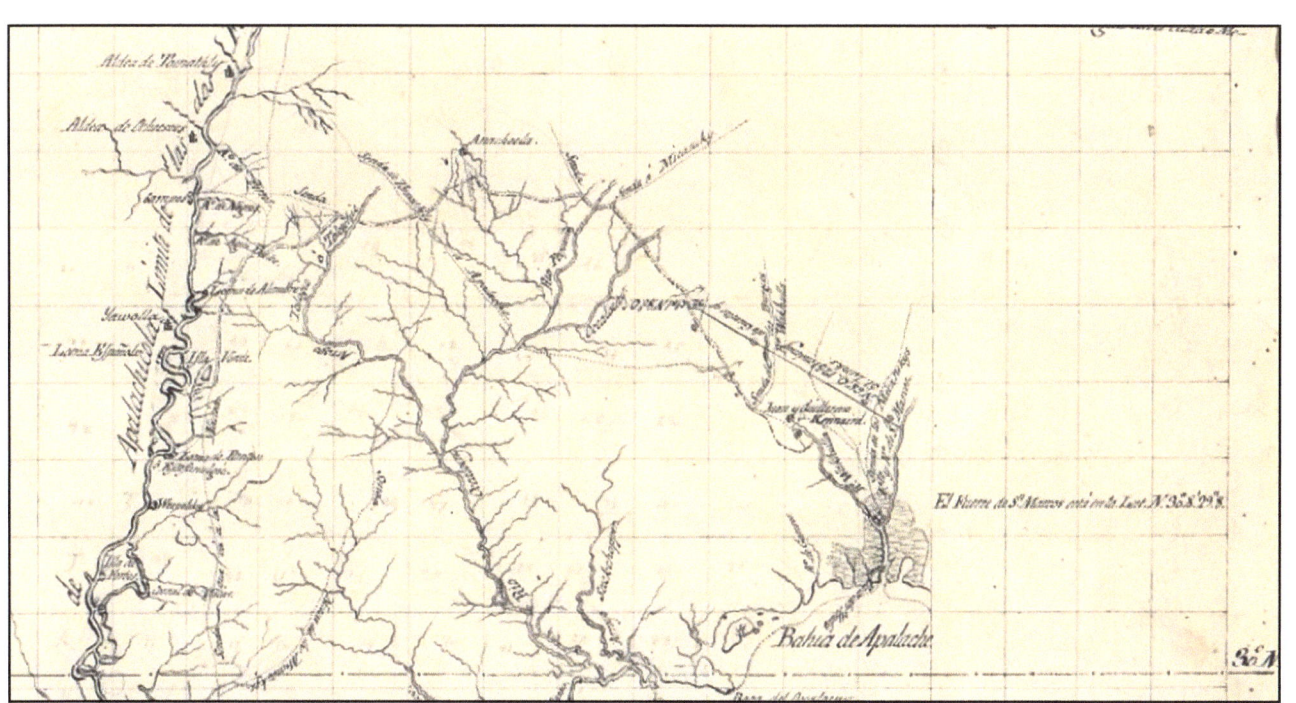

of Littman. This path passed beyond the headwaters of six or seven branches of Quincy Creek before joining the present U S Highway 90. Soon turning west, the old path crossed North Mosquito Creek

> "... a river which has 24 feet of width and 24 feet (sic) in depth in the rainy season and in the dry season has water to the knees of the horses."
>
> Delgado, October 30, 1686[59]

After approximately another two miles, the traveler reached the Apalachicola River. Here on the east bank was a village.

> "... on the bank of another large and copious river which takes its name from that province [Apalachicoli] and runs through it from north to south, is a heathen village called formerly Santa Cruz de Sabacola el Menor, now La Encarnacion a la Santa Cruz de Sabacola, the church having been dedicated to this sovereign mystery on Thursday, February 18th of this year, wherein have gathered the Great Cacique of that province, with his vassals from Sabacola el Grande which I have converted to our holy faith, ... " Bishop Calderon, 1676[60]

The Sabacola, also Savacola or Saucola, were living in Apalachicoli lands.

> "At the evening hour of prayer I reached the banks of the river called Apalachicola, which empties into the sea. That same night I, the reverend fathers, and several others crossed the stream in dugouts with considerable difficulty to a spot on the opposite side to spend the night because of the great discomfort of the east bank. This place they call the Choctaw village, and it is the most outlying mission [San Nicolas] port and curacy of his Majesty in this region."
>
> Ayala, June 9, 1693[61]

The late seventeenth century village and mission San Nicolas or perhaps San Carlos of the Chacatos Indians was located near the modern town of Sneads. The Christianized Chacatos appear to have moved here from their homeland to the west after 1675. Later in the eighteenth century the Seminole village of Tomatley was established near here.

---

58. Vincente Sebastian Pintado, Plano borrador De las Provincias de los Senores Forbes y Compania entre Los Rios Apalachicola y San Marcos en la Florida Occidental, ca. 1815, Papers of Vincente Sebastian Pintado, Container 15, Univ. of West Florida Library. The trail mentioned on this map translates "Thomson's Path to Apalachee". Perhaps it should be noted that on a circa 1818 map titled Map of a Part of West Florida (file in the Library of Congress), there is a trail labelled "Thompsons Path to Appalachy". It crossed the Little River where possibly Thomson's Path crossed, but seemed to run westward to Ocheesee on the Apalachicola River. The identity of Thomson and Thompson and their relation, if any, are unknown.

59. Boyd, "Expedition of Marco Delgado", 22

60. Calderon, "Florida and the Florida Missions", 7.

61. Leonard, "Journal of Don Laurenzo de Torres y Ayala", 230.

CHAPTER EIGHT

# The Road to Calistoble

*"Continuing on this course one league is the Rio de aPalache Colo [Apalachicola] that has 540 feet of width where it is joined by the Rio de Pedernales [Flint River] which has at its mouth 18 feet of depth and averages 5 palmos and at the landing place of a village of Christian Chacatos [Mission Santa Cruz de Sabacola] is 12 feet without being in flood. Departing from the village of the Chacatos to the northwest on the road to Calistoble there is encountered at 5 leagues a spring of clear water [Blue Springs in Jackson County, called by the Spaniards "Calistoble"] which forms a river that has 48 feet of width. At the spring it is 36 feet in depth and the river below is from one yard to one yard and one-half in depth and is bordered by thickets of large cane about six inches thick (une heme de grueso)."*

Delgado, 1686[62]

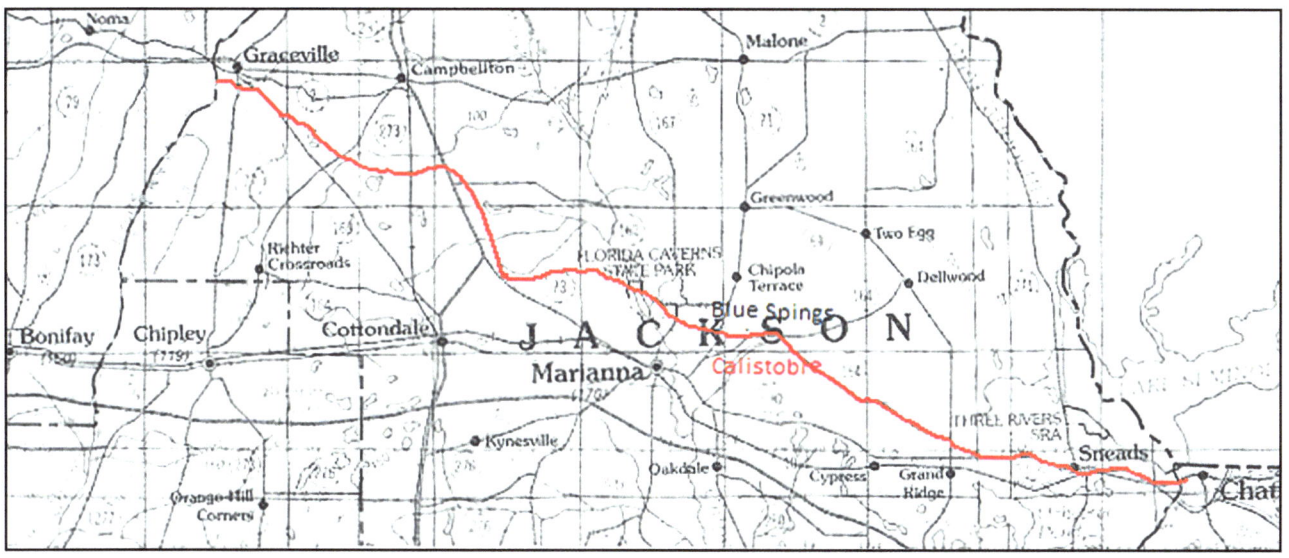

62. Boyd, "Expedition of Marcos Delgado", 22.

# THE ROAD TO CALISTOBLE

The old trail followed closely U. S. Highway 90. In Sneads, just south of Highway 90, the old road is still called "The Old Spanish Trail".

Approximately eight miles west of the Apalachicola the old road took a northwestwardly course to the spring of Calistoble (Fig. 35 & 36). Present Reddoch Road is a footprint of this trail (Fig. 34).

Friar Rodrigo de la Barreda, who accompanied Ayala on his expedition and who at times led an advance scouting party, described the springs.

*... we proceeded northwest through various woods and pine groves and, in about five leagues, reached such a large and excellent spring that a stream deep enough for canoes actually issues from it - the Indians sail on it. This stream joins the Apalachicola river a league more or less above where the latter empties into the sea [actually the stream joins the Chipola River, which in turn joins the Apalachicola]. This spring is entirely surrounded by woods with many walnut [hickory?], evergreen oak, laurel, common oak, sassafras, and some pine trees; around it are numerous huge rocks and habitable caves frequented by the Indians on their hunting trips for bear, deer, and buffalo, of which there is an abundance. The soil for three or four leagues round about is rich and suitable for all kinds of cultivation. There are very excellent wild grapes on the many vines, and many luscious chestnuts. Here we spent the night, thanking God for such a pleasant and delightful spot uninhabited save for the wild animals who enjoy it."*

Barreda, June 11, 1693[63]

---

63. Leonard, "Journal of Friar Rodrigo de la Barreda", 267

(Top Left) Figure 34: "...on the road to Calistoble." Reddoch Road, Jackson Co.

(Bottom Left) Figure 35: Old Spanish Trail interpretive sign and trace of the old road (right background), Blue Springs, Marianna.

THE ROAD TO CALISTOBLE

(Above) Figure 36: Blue Springs with Robinson Plantation visible in the distance. 1903. Courtesy State Archives of Florida, Florida Memory.

From the spring, Andrew Jackson's army marched six and a quarter miles to a natural crossing of the Chipola River.

*"The Natural Bridge is in the center of a large swamp and appears to be a deposit of earth on a raft or some similar obstruction. The passage is narrow and the creek, with a rapid current is visible both above and below."*

Young, 1818[64]

The Natural Bridge of the Chipola River, north of present Marianna, was indeed marshy.

*"In a short distance we ran into considerable difficulty in getting both the horses and men on foot through because of the many bogs, creeks, and woods; the horses became mired to their cinch straps, and the men on foot to their waists. However, our determination caused bridges and brush roads to be built so that we would keep moving forward on foot, with the unloaded horses falling and getting up again."*

Ayala, June 12, 1693[65]

64. Young, "Topographical Memoir of East and West Florida", no. 3, 153-154.

65. Leonard, "Journal of Don Laurenzo de Torres y Ayala", 230-231.

Somewhere west of the Natural Bridge and before Tanner Springs was the Arch Cave or Rockarch, as it was so called by the early American colonists. In Spanish times it was the 17th century Chacato village of Achercatane and short-lived mission site of San Nicolas de Tolentino, as was the village of Atanchia and mission San Carlos de Yatcatahi, the western most village, whose location has not been identified. One had also now entered the lands of the Chacatos, also known as the Chatots.[66]

*"Nine leagues from Encarnacion, on the northern frontier, is another [village] named San Nicolas, of about 30 inhabitants, and 3 leagues further on is another, San Carlos, of something like 100 inhabitants. Both these are of the Chacatos nation, which 14 years ago requested baptism and had not their desire fulfilled until the 21st of June of last year, 1674. In that section, living in encampments without any permanent dwellings, are more than 4,000 heathen called Chiscas, who sustain themselves with game, nuts and roots of trees."*

Bishop Calderon, 1675[67]

*" ... we reached an abandoned village of the Choctaw [actually the Chacatos] tribe called San Nicolas, where I came to preach the holy gospel in the year '74. Here we spent the night in the hollow of such a beautiful and unusual rock that I can state positively that more than 200 men could be lodged most comfortably within it; inside there is a brook which gushes from the living rock. It has plenty of light and height with three apertures buttressed by stonework of unusual natural architecture. Around it are level plots of ground, groves of trees and pine woods, all of which are delightful and with no other drawback than that of being uninhabited."*

Barreda, June 12, 1693[68]

Now on solid ground, both Ayala's and later Jackson's army marched to Holmes Creek. First, they proceeded north on what became the Territorial road to Campbellton, but now present Union Road. (Fig. 37) Turning northwest and following a course very similar to the present Jacob, Sharon, Peanut, Prim and Bony Bridge roads, their next obstacle was Holmes Creek. Perhaps somewhere along this route lay the unidentified site of Mission San Carlos.

---

66. For a thorough discussion of the two westernmost Chacato settlements and the revolts that occurred in that province, see John H. Hann, "The Chacato Revolt Inquiry", Visitations and Revolts in Florida, 1656-1695, Florida Archaeology, No. 7, 1993, 31-75

67. Calderon, "Florida and the Florida Missions", 7.

68. Leonard, "Journal of Friar Rodrigo de la Barreda", 267-268

(Above) Figure 37: Beyond the Road to Calistoble. Old Campbellton Road, north of Union-Jacob Roads intersection, Jackson Co.

CHAPTER NINE

# THE RED GROUND PATH

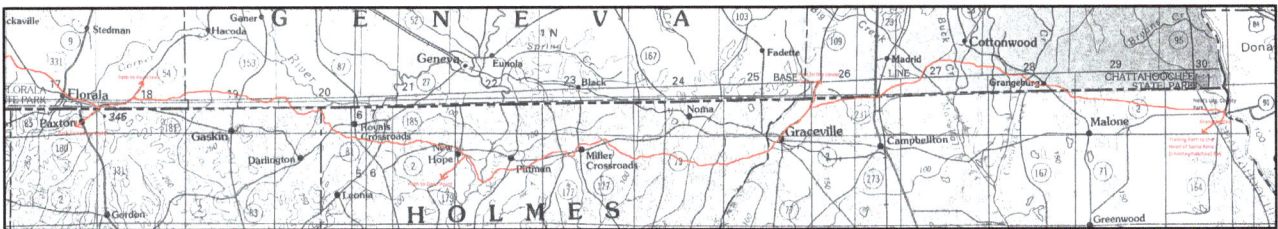

Returning to the village of Ekanachattee on the Chattahoochee River, the more northerly Red Ground Path went west, and wound in and out of Alabama and Florida. Leaving the village, the trail approximates Biscayne Road just north of Florida State Road 2. Then it turned northwest, and traversed the creeks that ultimately converge to form the Chipola River - namely from east to west, Cowarts Creek, Gum Slough, Boggy Branch, Buck Creek, Big Creek and Spring Creek. Portions of present Cottonwood and State Line roads may lie in the old trail's footprint. Descending back into Florida, Purcell's group mentions the village of Pokanaweethly or Coosa Old Fields, probably near Gaynor Pond. Here a trail to the north called by Purcell, the "Path to the Lower Creeks" merged with the Red Ground Path.

*"This day we arrived at a small settlement of Indians called the Cousah Old Fields, where we met with a friendly reception. All the chiefs being from home, we had not an opportunity of acquainting them with our business."*

Captain Holmes, July 23, 1778[69]

The trail continued southwest through present Graceville and then merged with the path that linked to the Road to Calistoble. Next was Holmes Creek, which Captain Young called "Okchiahatche" (River of the Okchai).

*"Okchiahatche is a branch of Choctahatche, [and] is thirty feet wide at the crossing place - with sandy bottom and banks and a narrow thicket."*

Young, 1818[70]

69. Jones, History of Decatur County, 62.

70. Young, "Topographical Memoir of East and West Florida", no. 3, 155.

The Okchai Indians were settled in the area in 1778 when Purcell's group passed through, but interestingly he refers to this creek as "Weekaywee Hatchee or Spring Creek", not as a river or creek of the Okchai. This Indian tribe was apparently replaced by 1818 by the Euchees.

Crossing Holmes Creek probably along present Bony Bridge Road or perhaps a little to the south, the Red Ground Path continued in a serpentine course crossing Wrights, Hurricane and many smaller creeks before reaching the Choctawhatchee River. This segment has little trace of the old road. Present Woodham, County Road 160, State Road 2, and Willoughby Lane may mirror the course of the old path.

*"I went and camped for the night by a deep river ... We found a baria(?) log already cut for a dugout, for it was impossible to ford the river. This boat was made and in this way we transferred all our supplies, saddles, and harness for the horses to the opposite bank while these beasts swam across, and thus we kept ferrying over. When this was accomplished, I left four Indians to guard the dugout for me until our return, God willing. I gave the name Santa Rosa [Choctawhatchee] to this stream."*

Ayala, June 16-20, 1693[71]

*"We ... went to Benjamin Steadham's Settlement where we got a fresh supply of provisions. [The next day] I was detained at Steadham's all this day, being seized with a violent fever ... "*

Holmes, July 20-21, 1778[72]

Benjamin Steadham was a trader among the Creek Indians. He resided at "Steadhams", located on the east side of the Choctawhatchee River and at present Curry's Ferry in Holmes County. Like so many other eighteenth century settlements, this was on an earlier settlement described as "Coosada Town in ruins" or more commonly called "Coosada Old Town." The old ferry crossing is now about two hundred yards north northeast of the current landing. The landing is plainly visible by a cut in the old bank behind the present owner, Wilmer Curry's home. Mr. Curry can remember the old landing and that sometime in the 1920's, a flood (probably the Hoover Flood of 1929) altered the river's course, thereby leaving the old landing well off the river and useless.[73]

Once across the river, the path took a north northwest course to Limestone Branch (Fig. 38). This segment is perhaps the best preserved part of the Red Ground Path. At Limestone Branch, Purcell showed a road to the southeast, called "Path to Deer Point". If the traveler took this path to the left, they would end on the east side of Pensacola Bay. This path closely followed the present Mt. Ida/Rum Road.

Travelers west of the Choctawhatchee seem to have had a difficult time navigating the trail.

---

71. Leonard, "Journal of Don Laurenzo de Torres y Ayala", 232.

72. Jones, History of Decatur County, 62

73. Wilmer Curry, interview by author April 15, 2006, Curry Ferry, P. O. Izagora, FL

" ... the guides with me declared that they did not know the way - a situation which gave me a good deal to think about and greatly depressed us all until I made up my mind to push west and west-southwest."

Ayala, June 16, 1693[74]

" ... the guide then left the trail and piloted us through the woods - twenty miles through a rolling pine country with numerous little reedy branches between the hills ... "

Young, 1818[75]

(Above) Figure 38: Primitive road west of Choctawhatchee River and Curry Ferry, Holmes Co.

74. Leonard, "Journal of Don Laurenzo de Torres y Ayala", 233.

Indian guides apparently had difficulty traversing this path. Purcell states that of all the segments of the Spanish Road, the Red Ground path was "small and little trod."[76] Many creeks and minor branches had to be crossed. These included Blackshire Creek, Camp Creek (Purcell's "Camp Branch"), and Hurricane Creek, where Hurricane Creek Road follows the old path.

Turning northwest, the path crossed Chestnut Creek (Purcell's "Fishing Creek") and then into Alabama. The route now hugged the Florida/Alabama border on the Alabama side, crossing Eightmile and Natural Bridge (Purcell's "Underground Creek") Creeks. Where it merged with present Alabama State Road 54, a fork to the northeast led along an Indian "Path to Pea Creek" according to Purcell. Hardly one mile beyond, another fork to the southwest led along the "Path to Yellow Water (Yellow River)", now present Teller Road. This path no doubt led down the ridge separating Pine Log and Pond Creeks.

Highway 54 follows the old path into the present town of Florala, skirting the north shore of Lake Jackson (Purcell's "Great Pond"). General Jackson's army is rumored to have camped on the lake's shore (Fig. 39).

The Red Ground Path took a more northwestward turn now in order to bypass the vast marsh created by the headwaters of Horseshoe Creek. At the most northern point of the trail, it terminated into the next segment of the road to Pensacola.

(Right) Figure 39: Andrew Jackson historical marker near Lake Jackson, Florala. Courtesy waymarking.com.

75. Young, "Topographical Memoir of East and West Florida", no. 3, 157.

76. Boyd, "Map of the Road from Pensacola to St. Augustine", 18.

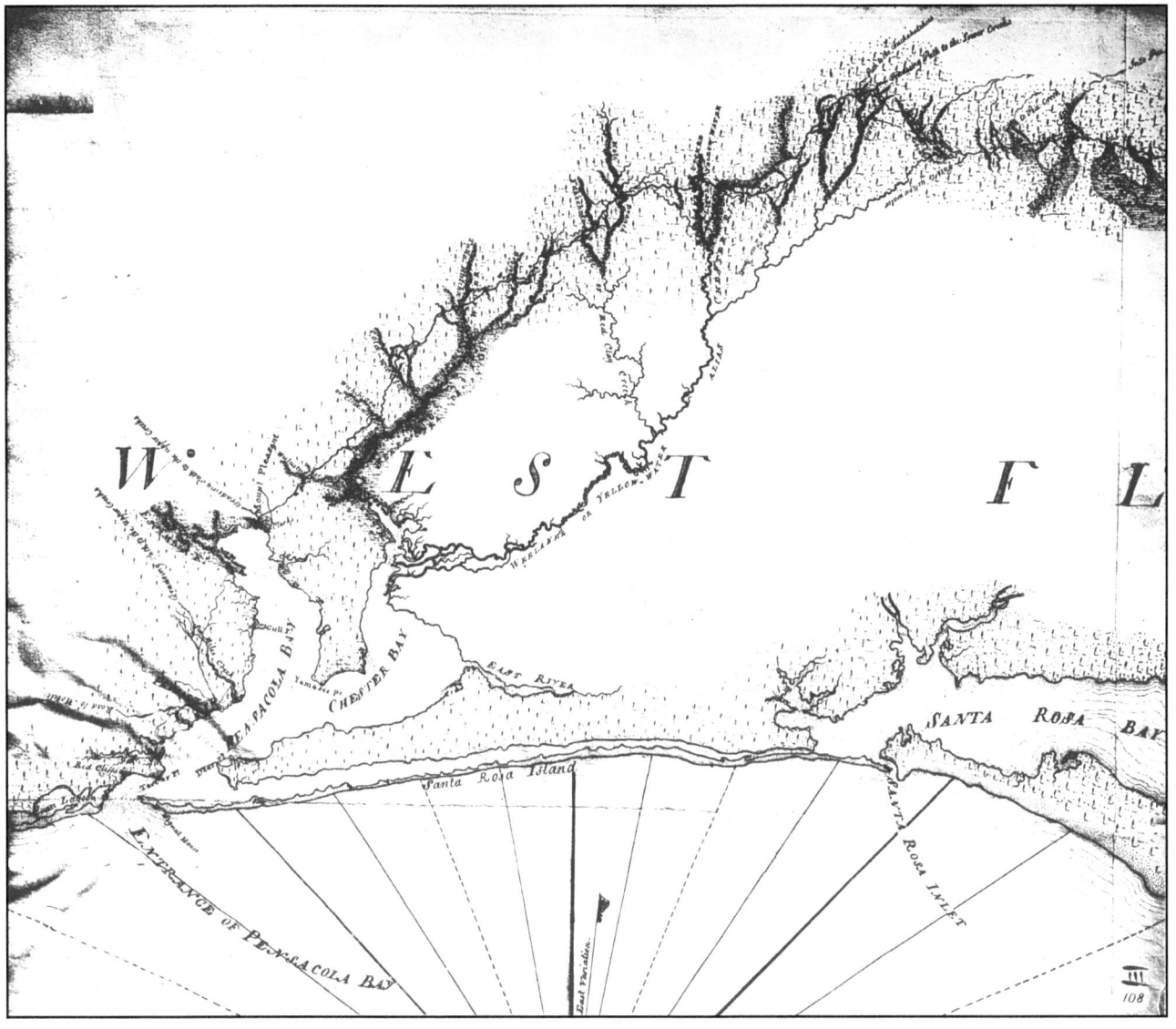

(Above) Figure 40: Joseph Purcell's 1778 *Map of the Road from Pensacola in West Florida to St. Augustine in East Florida* showing the Lower Creek Trading Path and the west extremity of the Red Ground Path. Courtesy National Archives, UK.

# CHAPTER TEN

# The Lower Creek Trading Path

*"The Path between Mount Pleasant [Floridatown] and the Fork of the Lower Creek Trading Path is plain and well trod, ..."*

Purcell, 1778[77]

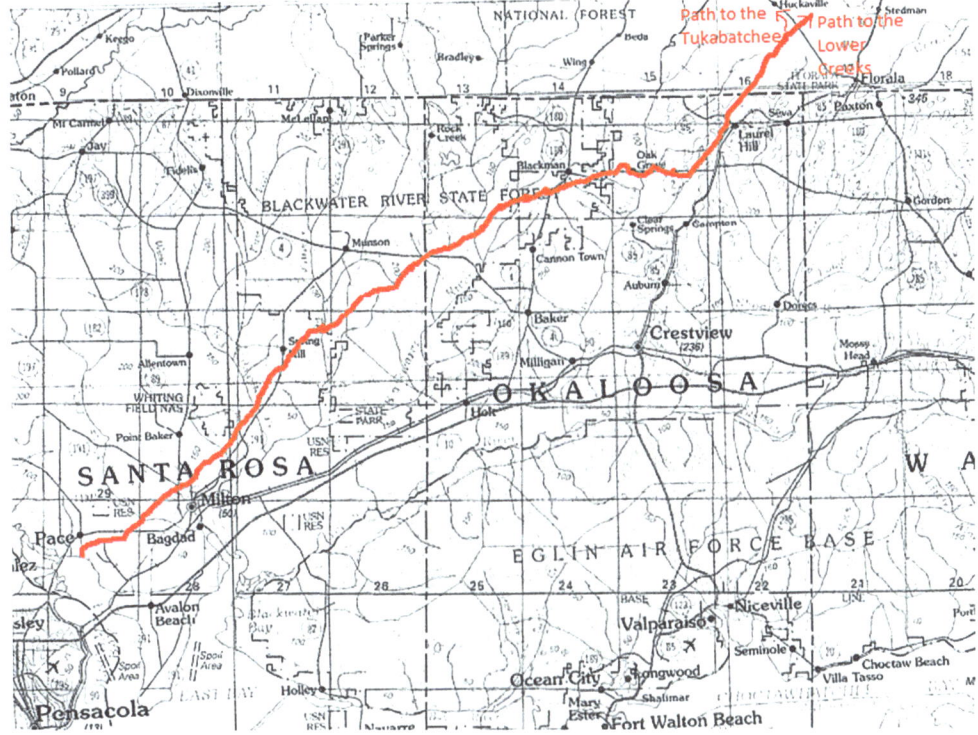

Unlike the other segments of the Spanish Road, the Lower Creek Trading Path (Fig. 40) is basically a north to south road with its Florida portion incorporated into the east-west road. It was a major route to the heartlands of the Lower Creeks in Georgia and also the Upper Creeks in Alabama. Hardly a mile to the west of the Path's junction with the Red Ground Path, the "Path to the Tukabatchees" forks to the north. The Upper Creek Tukabatchees were centered on the Tallapoosa River in present Elmore County.

Besides the accounts of the three travelers described below, there are the early American surveys done in the late 1820's and again partially done in 1851. These accurately plot the Trading Path all the way to Pensacola Bay. By their time, the path was designated "Jackson's Trail" or "General Jackson's Trail"

Turning south, the old trail entered Florida probably along present Thomas and Stokes roads, before passing through the western edge of present Laurel Hill. The trail then

77. *Ibid*

turned southwest and then west "to yellow water [Yellow River] along a high pine ridge dividing two of its tributary creeks [Murder and Mill Creeks]."[78]

Approximately three miles before the Yellow River, a Path to Deer Point forked to the south and followed the basin divide between Shoal and Yellow Rivers. This alternate path probably was incorporated into the nineteenth century Griffin Ferry Road, a connector road between Geneva, Alabama and Milton, Florida.

After being lost since leaving the Choctawhatchee River, Andrew Jackson's army may have found their way again east of Yellow River as the above quote from Captain Hugh Young seems to match the known terrain of the Trading Path (Fig. 41). The earlier Anglo/Creek military party of Capt. David Holmes and Purcell seemed to also be on the correct path. The third known army to have travelled this route, that of the Spanish Captain Don Luarenzo de Torres y Ayala, still seemed lost as evidenced in his journal.

Ayala did give descriptions of the features that he encountered. In approaching what may have been the Yellow River, he states:

*"I reached a beautiful and fairly broad river which we forded with the water rising to the horses' bellies. I called this stream San Juan river."*

Ayala, June 24, 1693[79]

Purcell gave the Native American name for the Yellow Water: "Weelanee", and commented that it is not fordable. He further states:

*"Weelanee has a large swamp on each side which is overflowed in the Freshes."*

Purcell, 1778[80]

(Right) Figure 41: "the path is plain and well trod." "General Jackson's Trail" East of Yellow River, Okaloosa Co

78. Young, "Topographical Memoir of East and West Florida", no. 3, 158

79. Leonard, "Journal of Don Laurenzo de Torres y Ayala", 233

80. Boyd, "Map of the Road from Pensacola to St. Augustine", 18

Figure 42: Yellow River Baptist Church Road, Okaloosa Co.

Young with Jackson's army stated that:

*"Yellow Water is twenty-five yards at the crossing place - has a bluff on the east side and a swamp a quarter of a mile wide on the west - the current is rapid and deep - the banks and bottoms sandy."*

Young, 1818[81]

*"Still pushing west, we crossed many creeks, the water of which was very clear and cold ... the branches and openings of these little streams [gave] us a good deal of trouble ..."*

Ayala, June 24, 1693[82]

*"All these streams are tributaries of Yellow Water[83] and are very similar in character and appearance. Their currents are rapid - beautifully clear and run in wide channels of the whitest sand. The banks mostly open and low with commonly a hill on one side and a glady flat stretching to a small distance on the other; ... "*

Young, 1818[84]

81. Young, "Topographical Memoir of East and West Florida", no. 3, 158.
82. Leonard, "Journal of Don Laurenzo de Torres y Ayala", 233.
83. Young, "Topographical Memoir of East and West Florida", no. 3, 159, was in error here. Only the first two "streams" encountered west of the Yellow River were tributaries, those being Big Horse and Polley Creeks. All the rest were tributaries of Blackwater River.
84. Young, "Topographical Memoir of East and West Florida", no. 3, 158.

It is hard to identify the branches, creeks and rivers that Ayala and Purcell now encountered as they traveled west and southwest (Fig. 42). Captain Young however gives such accurate distances to these waterways that it is easy to identify them: 2.5 miles to " ... a small creek with steep banks and very miry on the west side [Big Horse Creek]" and 1 mile to " ... a miry branch [Polley Creek]". Continuing, he stated:

*"The country is then rolling, the path running on a ridge for five miles to a creek twelve feet wide with open high banks and sandy bottom."* Young, 1818[85]

*"We came upon a creek which it was necessary to skirt south along its banks because of the many flooded stretches..."*

Ayala, June 24, 1693[86]

Young referred to present-named Panther Creek, known by Purcell as Mole Branch. The earlier traveler Ayala may have referred to this creek in his above statement.

Just before Panther Creek, the Florida Trail Association has built a hiking path, which approximates the Trading Path. Named the "Jackson Red Ground Florida Trail", it is in the Blackwater River State Forest (Fig. 43).

As correctly measured by Young, it was four miles to the Blackwater River, Purcell's Red Clay Creek or Futeechattelagga. The 1828 U. S. survey calls it the "East Fork of Black Water". Ayala referred to it by yet another name.

*" ... I came upon a stream which the Indians call the Colorado River. Numerous buffalo tracks were found on its banks; in the river itself were many fishes of all kinds by which our whole outfit was refreshed."*

Ayala, June 25, 1693[87]

Ayala continued, apparently either lost or building the road.

*"I continued for two leagues through numerous thickets, making bridges and brush roads ... "*

Ayala, June 26, 1693[88]

Young records Jackson's march onwards: 2 miles to " ... a small miry branch (East Prong of Muddy Branch)", a quarter of a mile to " ... a large branch with open but miry banks (West Prong of Muddy Branch)", and three quarters of a mile to " ... a large branch of the same character (Beaver Creek)". As for Ayala, he continued through several cane brakes, building brush roads and bridges.

---

85. Ibid.
86. Leonard, "Journal of Don Laurenzo de Torres y Ayala", 233.
87. Ibid.
88. Leonard, "Journal of Don Laurenzo de Torres y Ayala", 234.

The Path now continued southwest along a low ridge which separates the tributaries of Blackwater River from the tributaries of Sweet Water Creek. This "gap" or "pass" between the branches seemed to have a name. Purcell called it "Boggy Cut".

Jackson's army marched another 6.5 miles to " ... a large creek with high steep hills on the east and a palmetto flat on the west ... ". This was Purcell's "Palmetto Creek" or "Tallahatchee", which is present Big Juniper Creek. Here is the western boundary of the Blackwater River State Forest and the terminus of the Jackson Red Ground hiking trail. The 1828 survey referred to the creek as Sweet Water, which is today the name of one of Big Juniper's major branches further north. Purcell and Ayala indicate it was not fordable. Ayala states:

" ... I came upon a river; as soon as we had crossed it, we by a bridge and the horses by swimming, we again marched on ... "

Ayala, June 28, 1693[89]

Young with Jackson continued 1.25 miles to " ... a branch of ten feet wide and sandy bottom (Maria Branch)." Then 5.25 miles to " ... a large creek sixty feet wide, open on the east side and with a narrow thicket on the west - a good ford was found a quarter mile below the path." This was Coldwater Creek, Purcell's unfordable "Cold Water" or "Weekasupka", and the 1828 survey's "West Fork of Black Water".

Continuing southwest:

"Two and a half miles [to] another creek with low open banks and sandy bottom - the bottom uneven and somewhat obstructed at the ford by logs ... "

Young, 1818[90]

(T0-) Figure 43: Author Bob Hurst on the Jackson Trail, Blackwater River State Forest, Santa Rosa Co.

89. Ibid
90. Young, "Topographical Memoir of East and West Florida", no. 3, 159.

This was Clear Creek, or Clear Water River according to the 1828 and 1851 surveys. In 1778, Purcell named it "Clear Water" or "Weehiheaga" and stated it not fordable. Ayala announced a rather puzzling discovery:

*"I had news from the reverend father [Friar Rodrigo de la Barreda, a member of the expedition] that he had discovered a mountain which appeared to be split by some river."*

Ayala, June 29, 1693[91]

It is hard to determine exactly Ayala's location. He was lost. The next day he states:

*"We kept traveling southwest, south and southeast, with the mountain always in sight. We became so confused that, when I noticed the directions that we were taking, I saw that we were retracing our way; and so, after traveling six leagues, I pitched camp on the bank of a creek with everyone in a state of the utmost discouragement."*

Ayala, June 30, 1693[92]

What "mountain" he referred to is indeed puzzling. The highest elevation around Clear and Pond Creeks is 170 feet. Tracking his journey, it would seem logical to assume that the river dividing the mountain would be Clear Creek, because he mentioned his encounter with another creek after this. The only major waterway after Clear Creek and before the bay is Pond Creek, aka Weelustee or Black Water according to Purcell.
Young continued:

*" ... five and three quarter miles to a creek twenty feet wide with high open banks and sandy bottom and a high hill with red sandstone on the east side and a flat with some palmetto on the west."*

Young, 1818[93]

The red sandstone is still visible, as is evidenced at the archaeological site of Arcadia Mill on Pond Creek. It is an "ironstone", known for its high iron content that gives it a reddish hue. The stone was quarried in the late 1820's.

Young records that from Pond Creek to Escambia Bay there was a distance of 4.5 miles (Fig. 44). In 1693, Ayala sent out soldiers to reconnoiter.

---

91. Leonard, "Journal of Don Laurenzo de Torres y Ayala", 235.
92. Ibid
93. Young, "Topographic Memoir of East and West Florida", no. 3, 159.

" ... though their horses got deeply mired; the soldiers returned a little more than two hours after their departure with the glad tidings that they had seen this river [Escambia] and that it was quite broad and deep with high bluffs and many flooded mudflats and swamps along its edges."

Ayala, July 1, 1693[94]

They had reached the impenetrable marsh delta of the Escambia River, with its many fingers flowing into the bay. Extending into the twentieth century a ferry service had to be used to convey travelers and commerce from Pensacola around the delta to higher ground near present Floridatown.

Ayala also sent out five Apalachee guides to reconnoiter to the south. After two days:

" ... they brought word that they had seen the bay and its landmarks, and had been on the spot where the Pensacola Indians once had their village. This last item of news I did not receive with pleasure as I knew by it that no Indians were there, and this discovery was what I was most concerned about; nor was there any explanation of what had become of them."

Ayala, July 1, 1693[95]

(Above) Figure 44: Primitive Trail, Pace.

94. Leonard, "Journal of Don Laurenzo de Torres y Ayala", 235-236.

95. Leonard, "Journal of Don Laurenzo de Torres y Ayala", 236.

Ayala's party now advanced south.

*"I came to the edge of this great bay about a quarter of a league from the delta formed by the river [Escambia]. I pitched camp and at once gave the order to cut down a pine tree to make a dugout ... I went and dismounted from my horse on the very site formerly occupied by the Pensacolas and found there the ruins of their huts; these are now being used for the shacks we are building to shelter and protect us from the sun and rain."*

Ayala, July 2, 1693[96]

The "Penzacolas" may have been an indigenous tribe, eliminated perhaps by the Yamassee and Creek slavers, and by the continuous wars with the neighboring Movilas on Mobile Bay.

Although all indications are that Ayala found utter desolation along the north shore of Escambia Bay, this was not the case by 1778. Purcell shows either a community or plantation near the bay called "Mt. Pleasant." David Holmes, himself, may have had a farm near here. On the arrival of General Jackson's army, Young writes:

*"Settlements are scattered along the shore from this point [Floridatown] to the mouth of the Yellow Water Bay and among them are some handsome and productive plantations of second rate land."*[97]

---

96. Leonard, "Journal of Don Laurenzo de Torres y Ayala", 236-237

97. Young, "Topographical Memoir of East and West Florida", no. 3, 159.

## CHAPTER ELEVEN

# END OF THE TRAIL

The deterioration of the old Spanish Road parallels the demise of the Spanish missions. In 1824, Captain Daniel Burch had trouble locating any trace of the old road during his visit to San Luis. With the United States acquisition of Florida in 1819 and its subsequent American colonization, the changes in settlement patterns precipitated a change in the road system. The building of the Military or Federal Road in 1824 was an attempt to shorten and replace the old Spanish Road. In West Florida, this new road and several others, such as the Pensacola to Geneva Road and the Holmes Valley Road, certainly contributed to the abandonment of much of the Red Ground Path. On the other hand, in the east, that part of the Military Road, commonly called the Old St. Augustine or Bellamy Road, actually preserved many parts of the older road.

Nevertheless, the old road was never forgotten. As has been pointed out before, the 1926 U. S. Highway 90 was labelled "The Old Spanish Trail". In the town of Sneads, a portion of the old road is still called "The Old Spanish Trail". In Suwannee County, near Ichetucknee Springs, a portion of a road in called "The Old Spanish Road". Portions of current roads and hiking trails that are named in the appendices below will keep the memory of the old road alive for many centuries to come.

# APPENDIX I

# Points of Interest

### ST. JOHNS COUNTY

St. Augustine
Bartram Trail Historic Marker

### CLAY COUNTY

Bayard Road, Bayard Conservation Area
Bellamy Road Historic Marker

### PUTNAM COUNTY

Banana/Melrose Cemetery Historic Marker

### ALACHUA COUNTY

Springhill Methodist Church, Traxler and Historic Marker

### COLUMBIA COUNTY

Oleno State Park

### SUWANNEE COUNTY

Ichetucknee Springs State Park
Little River Springs
Little River Springs Conservation Area
Royal Spring
Cow Spring
Wes Skiles Peacock Springs State Park
Charles Spring Conservation Area

### JEFFERSON COUNTY

Letchworth-Love Mounds Archaeological State Park

### LEON COUNTY

Shrine of the Martyrs (proposed)
De Soto Winter Encampment Site
Historic Marker
Mission San Luis

### DECATUR COUNTY, GA

El Camino Real & DeSoto Trail
Historic Markers
Cyrene Historic Marker

### GADSDEN COUNTY

Joshua Davis House
United States Arsenal
Ellicott's Observatory Historic Marker

### JACKSON COUNTY

Mission San Carlos Interpretive Kiosk, Sneads
Blue Springs Recreational Area
Florida Caverns State Park
Neal's Landing County Park

### HOLMES COUNTY

Keith Cabin Historic Marker
Wallace Williams Pioneer Home

### WALTON COUNTY

Alford's Mill Historic Marker

### COVINGTON COUNTY, AL

Andrew Jackson Historical Marker

### SANTA ROSA COUNTY

Blackwater River State Forest
Arcadia Mill Archaeological Site

## APPENDIX II

# Auto and Hiking Tours

For the readers that would like to venture out to get a feel for what the Spanish Road was like, there are several passable roads, and for the more realistic experience, several hikeable trails.

**BAYARD ROAD**, *Bayard Conservation Area, Green Cove Springs, Clay County:* The western most part of the road is through a beautiful hard wood forest, with overhanging, moss covered oaks and beautiful wild flowers. The middle section is through a planted pine forest. The eastern part is private.

**BELLAMY ROAD**, *off Bardin/Hogarth Roads, Clay County:* A primitive road necessitates a rugged vehicle. This road will give the traveler an idea of the difficulty the early travelers experienced in the marshy Eastern Valley.

**BELLAMY ROAD**, *Alachua County:* This beautiful canopy road was built by John Bellamy in 1824, and, though not exactly in the footprint of the Spanish Road, closely approximates it.

**OLENO STATE PARK** *(Fig. 45), Columbia County:* Nowhere else will the hiker get a better feel for the Spanish Road. The southeastern half of the Dogwood Trail (blazed in gray) gives one the experience of the deep furrows in parts of the Spanish Road. Paraner's Trail (blazed in green) to the southeast preserves the road better than any other hiking trail. Continue southeast to the park's boundary fence. These last two segments were part of the old Alligator Road of the 19th Century.

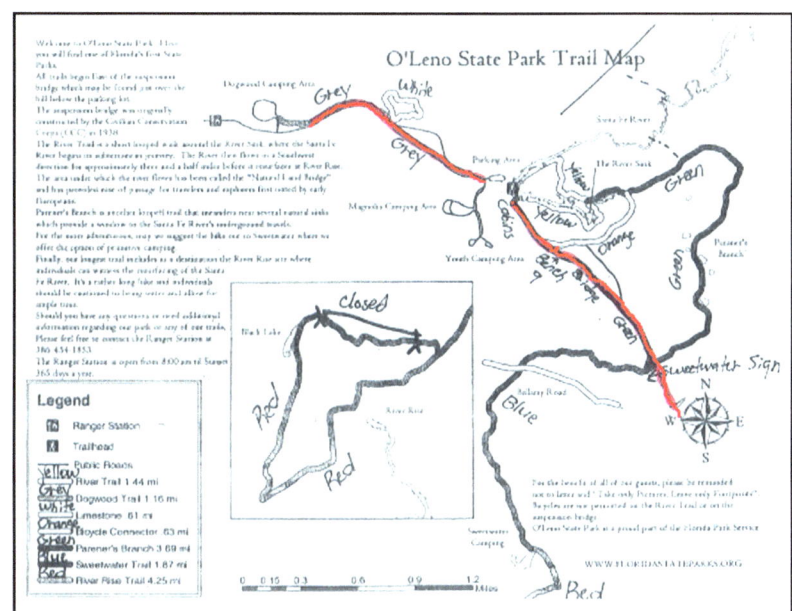

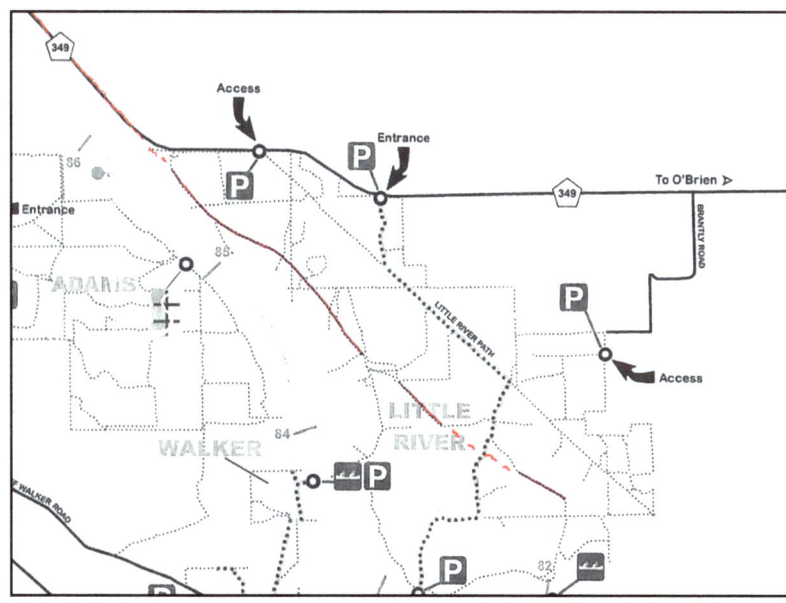

**LITTLE RIVER SPRINGS CONSERVATION AREA** *(Fig. 46), Suwannee County:* A primitive road, running parallel to the river and in the middle of the area from northwest to southeast, especially in the northwest section, gives the hiker an idea of what the

(Top) Figure 45: The Picolata Path (marked in red) in Oleno State Park, Columbia Co.

(Bottom) Figure 46: The Picolata Path (marked in red), a segment of the Spanish Road,

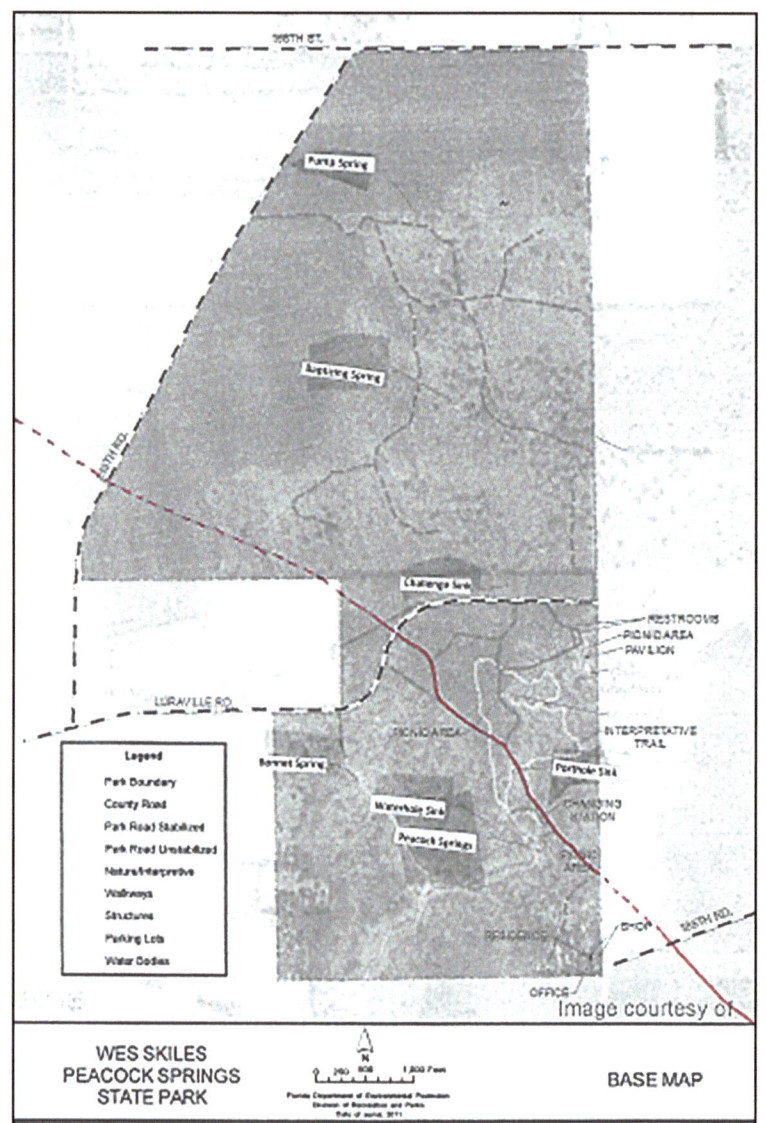

(Above) Figure 47: The Picolata Path (marked in red) in Wes Skiles Peacock Springs State Park, Suwannee Co.

early writers meant by "Broad Roads."

**WES SKILES PEACOCK SPRINGS STATE PARK** *(Fig. 47), Suwannee County:* Though emphasis at the park is on diving and the intricate subterranean cave system, there is a trail running southeast from the main parking lot to the park's boundary fence. The trail is marked "Staff Only". For permission to hike this short stretch contact Amy Conyers, Park Mgr., 18081 185th Road, Live Oak, FL 32060, tel. 386-776-2194. Northwest of the parking lot is an unmarked trail that runs northwest across 180th Street, and may have been built over by a railroad bed, still visible in the northwest corner area of the park.

**CHARLES SPRING CONSERVATION AREA,** *Suwannee County:* A designated and short "Bellamy Trail" for hiking only runs from the parking area to the graded road.

**HIKE LAKE ROAD,** *Madison County:* This rough graded road gives the traveler an idea of the marshy conditions experienced along the Spanish Road.

**OLD ST. AUGUSTINE ROAD,** *Jefferson County:* This graded road, paralleling to the south U. S. Highway 27, is now much wider than the old Spanish Road, but nevertheless gives the traveler some idea of the beautiful canopy of trees along this portion of the road.

**OLD BAINBRIDGE ROAD,** *Leon County:* This paved, deeply furrowed and beautiful canopied road closely follows the Spanish Road to the northwest of Tallahassee.

**BLUE SPRINGS RECREATIONAL AREA,** *Jackson County:* As at Charles Springs Conservation Area, there is a short walking trail designated "Old Spanish Trail" on the interpretive sign nearby.

**FLORIDA JACKSON RED GROUND TRAIL,** *Santa Rosa County:* Part of the Florida Trail, this hiking path mirrors the trek of Andrew Jackson's, David Holmes', and Ayala's armies as they marched along the Lower Creek Trading Path through pine ridges, rolling hills, and clear, sandy bottomed streams and rivers.

## APPENDIX III

# Places and Roads Along the Spanish Trail

## FROM ST. AUGUSTINE TO PENSACOLA

For those who might wish to do a combination drive and hike across the Spanish Trail, here is a suggested itinerary that would approximate the route of the Holmes-Purcell expedition:

### ST. JOHNS CO.

St. Augustine - County Road 208 - Glimpse of Glory - Picolata

### CLAY CO.

Bayard Conservation Area (Bayard Road)-Bellamy Road-White Sands Road-Keystone Heights – County Road 219

### ALACHUA CO.

Melrose – State Road 26 - Orange Heights - Austin Cary Memorial Forest - Traxler - Alligator Road

### COLUMBIA CO.

Oleno State Park - Elim Church Road - Ichetucknee Springs

### SUWANNEE CO.

Old Spanish Road or Bibbey Road - Little River Springs - Little River Springs Conservation Area - Peacock Springs - New Harmony Road - Charles Spring

### LAFAYETTE CO.

Ezell Landing - Mayo Junction

### MADISON CO.

County Road 53 - Pine Lake Road - Hike Lake Road - Hopewell - Sampala Lake – Sundown Creek Road (remains of Spanish causeway) - Aucilla Lookout Tower - US90 bridge over Aucilla River

### JEFFERSON CO.

Casa Blanca – U. S. Hwy 90 at Lake Miccosukee

### LEON CO.

Sunray Road – U. S. Hwy 90 - Wadesboro-Baum Road - Gardner - Tallahassee - San Luis Mission - Old Bainbridge Road - US27 bridge on Ochlocknee River

### GADSDEN CO.

Gibson - Scotland (Mission Escambe?) - Shady Rest - Littman – County Road 270 – Howell Road - Mt. Pleasant - Oak Grove – U. S. Highway 90 - Chattahoochee

### JACKSON CO.

Old Spanish Trail in Sneads - Reddoch Road - Blue Springs - Florida Caverns State Park - Blue Hole Spring - Dothan Hwy. - Union Road – Jacob Road – Sharon Road – Peanut Road – Prim Road - bridge across Holmes Creek south of Graceville

### HOLMES CO.

County Road 160 - Miller Crossroads - Pittman - Curry Ferry - Barton Road - New Hope - Commander Road - Hurricane Creek Road - Royals Crossroads Walton/Geneva Co., AL Boundary Natural Bridge - Gary Barker Road - Alafis Road

### COVINGTON CO., AL

Florala - Lockhart - Union Church Road

### OKALOOSA CO.

Laurel Hill - Oak Grove - Blackman - High Bridge Road

### SANTA ROSA CO.

Jackson Trail, Blackwater River State Forest - Spring Hill – in-between Serenity Gardens & Milton - Pea Ridge - Pace - Floridatown

# BIBLIOGRAPHY

Boyd, Mark. "A Map of the Road from Pensacola to St. Augustine, 1778". *Florida Historical Quarterly 17,* no. 1 (July 1938): 15-24.

Boyd, Mark. "Diego Pena's Expedition to Apalachee and Apalachicolo in 1716". *Florida Historical Quarterly 28,* no. 1 (July 1949): 1-27.

Boyd, Mark. "Expedition of Marcos Delgado, 1686". *Florida Historical Quarterly 16*, no. 1 (July 1937): 2-32.

Boyd, Mark F., Hale G. Smith and John W. Griffin. *Here They Once Stood, The Tragic End of the Apalachee Missions.* Gainesville: University of Florida Press, 1951.

Calderon, Gabriel Diaz Vara. "Florida and the Florida Missions". *A 17th Century Letter of Gabriel Diaz Vara Calderon, Bishop of Cuba, Describing the Indians and Indian Missions of Florida.* Translated by Lucy L. Wenhold. Washington: Smithsonian Institution, Nov. 20, 1936.

Carmody, John M. *The Spanish Missions of Florida.* Washington: The Administrative Federal Works Agency, 1940.

Chatelain, Verne E. *The Defense of Spanish Florida 1565-1763.* Washington: Carnegie Institution of Washington, Publication 611, 1941.

Ewen, Charles R. and John H. Hann. *Hernando de Soto among the Apalachee: The Archaeology of the First Winter Encampment.* Gainesville: University Press of Florida, 1998.

Hann, John H. *A History of the Timucua Indians and Missions.* Gainesville: University of Florida Press, 1996.

Hann, John H. *Visitations and Revolts in Florida, Florida Archaeology, 1656-1695*, No. 7, 1993.

Hooper, Keven. *Early History of Clay County: A Wilderness that could be tamed.* Charleston: The History Press, 2006.

Jones, Frank S. *History of Decatur County,* Georgia. Spartanburg: The Reprint Co., 1980.

Leonard, Irving. "Journal of Don Laurenzo de Torres y Ayala from the Expedition he made overland from San Luis de Apalachee to the Bay of Pensacola in the year of 1693, August 5, 1693". *Spanish Approach to Pensacola, 1689-1693.* Albuquerque: The Quivira Society, 1939.

Leonard, Irving. "Journal of Friar Rodrigo de la Barreda". *Spanish Approach to Pensacola, 1689-1693.*

Milanich, Jerald T. and Charles Hudson. *Hernando de Soto and the Indians of Florida.* Gainesville: University of Florida Press, 1993.

"National Register Testing at Neal's Landing." www.earth-search.com/NEALS.htm.

Pintado, Vincente Sebastian. *Plano borrador De las Provincias de los Senores Forbes y Compania entre Los Rios Apalachicola y San Marcos en la Florida Occidental,* ca. 1815. The Papers of Vincente Sebastian Pintado, Container 15 in the University of West Florida Library.

Vega, Garcilaso de la. *Florida of the Inca.* www.floridahistory.com/inca-5.html.

Vega, Garcilaso de la. *The Florida of the Inca.* Translated by John Grier Varner & Jeannette Johnson Varner. Austin: University of Texas Press, 1951.

Vignoles, Charles B. *Observations upon the Floridas.* New York: E. Bliss & E. White, 1823.

Young, Captain Hugh. "A Topographical Memoir on East and West Florida with itineraries of General Jackson's Army, 1818". *Florida Historical Quarterly* 13, no. 1 (July 1934): 16-50; no. 2 (Oct. 1934): 82-104; no. 3 (Jan. 1935): 129-164.

# INDEX

## A

| | |
|---|---|
| Afanochua | *39* |
| Afanoyvitachir | *32* |
| Aguacalyquen | *39* |
| Alabama State Road 54 | *36* |
| Alachua | *1, 17, 25, 32, 34, 36, 37, 83, 85, 87* |
| Alachua Trail | *36* |
| Alafis Road | *88* |
| Alford's Mill Historic Marker | *83* |
| Alligator Creek | *43* |
| Alligator Road | *37, 84, 86* |
| Amaca (lake) | *36* |
| Amarillo River | *54* |
| Anhaica | *52* |
| Apalachee Path | *22* |
| Apalachicoli Indians | *54, 60* |
| Aquilachua | *39* |
| Arcadia Mill | *78, 83* |
| Arch Cave | *65* |
| Arredondo, Antonio de | *31* |
| Atanchia | *65* |
| Atchercatane | *65* |
| Ates Creek | *32* |
| Attapulgus Creek | *55* |
| Aucilla Lookout Tower | *87* |
| Aucilla River | *11, 22, 35, 43-44, 49* |
| Austin Cary Memorial Forest | *87* |
| Avendano, Governor | *33* |
| Aviles, Pedro Menendez de | *27* |
| Ayala, Don Laurenzo de Torres y | *13-14* |

## B

| | |
|---|---|
| Bainbridge | *17-18, 21-22, 47, 55-56* |
| Baptizing Spring | *18, 39-40* |
| Bardin Road | *85* |
| Barton Road | *88* |
| Barnard, Timothy | *47* |
| Barreda, Rodrigo de la | *13* |
| Bartram Trail Historic Marker | *83* |
| Bartram, William | *30* |
| Baum Road | *87* |
| Bayard Conservation Area | *83, 85, 87* |
| Bayard Point | *30-31* |
| Bayard Road | *17, 83, 85, 87* |
| Beaver Creek | *76* |
| Bellamy, John | *34, 48, 45* |
| Bellamy Road | *1, 13, 25, 34, 36-38, 43, 46, 49* |
| Bellamy Road Historic Marker | *17, 34, 83* |
| Betton Road | *52* |
| Bibbey Road | *87* |
| Big Creek | *67* |
| Big Horse Creek | *76* |
| Big Juniper Creek | *77* |
| Biscayne Road | *67* |
| Blackman | *88* |
| Blackshire Creek | *70* |
| Black Water | *78* |
| Blackwater River State Forest | *76-77, 83, 88* |
| Blue Hole Spring | *87* |
| Blue Springs | *19, 23-24, 61, 63-64, 83, 86-87* |
| Boggy Branch | *67* |
| Boggy Cut | *77* |
| Bony Bridge Road | *65, 68* |
| Boyd, Mark | *21* |
| Bradford Road | *52* |
| Brinson | *47* |
| Bruff, James Goldsborough | *36* |
| Buck Creek | *67* |
| Burch, Daniel | *81* |
| Burgess | *22* |
| Burgess, James | *47* |

## C

| | |
|---|---|
| Calacala | *39* |
| Calderon, Gabriel Diaz Vara | *13* |

# INDEX

Calistoble ............................................................. 23-24
Campbellton ................................................. 19, 65-66
Camp Branch ............................................................ 70
Camp Creek .............................................................. 70
Capole ...................................................................... 51
Casa Blanca ............................................................. 46
Center Path ........................................... 22, 45, 49-54
Chacato Indians ...................................................... 23
Charles Spring ........................................................ 40
Charles Reuben ....................................................... 40
Chattahoochee River ...................... 22-24, 56-57, 67
Chatot Indians ................................................... 23, 65
Chipola River ........................................ 22-23, 62, 64, 67
Chestnut Creek ........................................................ 70
Chisca Indians .................................................... 54, 65
Chitonavajuno ........................................................ 39
Choctawhatchee River .......................... 19, 57, 68-69, 74
Clear Creek .............................................................. 78
Cockee ..................................................................... 57
Cody Escarpment ............................................... 49-50
Coldwater Creek ...................................................... 77
Colorado River ........................................................ 76
Commander Road .................................................... 88
Coosada Old Town .................................................. 68
Coosa Old Fields ..................................................... 67
Cottonwood ............................................................ 67
County Road 53 ....................................................... 87
County Road 160 ............................................... 68, 88
County Road 208 ..................................................... 87
County Road 219 ..................................................... 87
County Road 270 ..................................................... 87
Cowarts Creek ......................................................... 67
Cow Spring ......................................................... 40, 83
Creek of Ybitachuco ................................................ 50
Curry Ferry ........................................... 19, 68-69, 88
Curry, Wilmer .......................................................... 68
Cypress Grove .......................................................... 30
Cyrene Historic Marker .......................................... 83

## D

Delgado, Marcos ............................... 13, 54, 59-61, 89
Dell ........................................................................... 36
De Soto, Hernando ............. 1, 13, 35-37, 41, 49, 51, 89
De Soto Trail ....................................................... 36-37
De Soto Trail Historic Marker .............................. 83

De Soto Winter Encampment Site Historic Marker .... 83
Dogtown Road ......................................................... 55
Dogwood Trail ......................................................... 38
Donalsonville Road ................................................. 56
Dothan Highway ..................................................... 87
Drifton – Aucilla Highway ..................................... 46

## E

Eastern Valley ..................................................... 27, 85
East Fork of Black Water ........................................ 76
Ebb ........................................................................... 49
Eightmile Creek ....................................................... 70
Ekanachattee ................................................. 24, 57, 67
El Camino Real Historic Marker ........................ 17, 21
Ellicott's Observatory Historic Marker ................. 83
Elim Church Road ................................................... 38
El Pajon ............................................................... 29-30
Escambe .............................................................. 54, 87
Escambia Bay ............................................... 24, 78, 80
Escambia River .................................................. 24, 79
Ezell's Landing ................................................... 41-42

## F

Federal Road ................................ 13, 34, 43, 46, 50
Fig Spring ................................................................ 38
Fishing Creek .......................................................... 70
Fish Pond Drain ....................................................... 56
Five Mile Swamp ..................................................... 29
Flint River ............................................. 22-23, 48, 55, 61
Florala ........................................................ 19, 70, 88
Florida Caverns State Park .............................. 83, 87
Florida Santa Fe Trail ............................................ 36
Floridatown ............................................. 73, 79-80, 88
Florencia, Juan Fernandez de ........................... 13, 54
Fort Mosey ........................................................ 17, 28
Four Mile Swamp .................................................... 29
Fowlstown Road ..................................................... 55
Futeechattelagga (Creek) ....................................... 76

## G

Gardner .................................................................... 87
Gary Barker Road .................................................... 88
Gator Bone Lake ...................................................... 35
Gaynor Pond ............................................................ 67
Geneva ................................................................ 74, 81

George's Lake ................................................ *32, 35*
Gibson............................................................... *87*
Glimpse of Glory.......................................... *30, 87*
Godfrey, Mr. .................................................... *33*
Graceville.................................................... *67, 87*
Great Savannah Okaheepee............................... *54*
Great Pond................................................. *35, 70*
Green's Creek ................................................. *32*
Griffin Ferry Road ............................................ *74*
Guihenayoa...................................................... *43*
Gum Slough..................................................... *67*

### H

Hall Lake .................................................... *35-36*
Hammock of San Pedro .................................... *49*
Harmonia Path.........................................*22, 47-48*
Hatchet Creek ................................................. *36*
Hekopockee .................................................... *36*
Hicks Lake ...................................................... *47*
High Bridge Road ............................................ *88*
Highway 54...................................................... *70*
Hike Lake Road ............................................... *86*
Hixtown Swamp .............................................. *43*
Hogarth Road .................................................. *85*
Holmes, David .. *13, 33, 45, 47, 55-57, 68, 74, 80, 86-87*
Holmes Creek ................................ *23-24, 65, 67-68*
Holmes Valley Road ......................................... *81*
Hoover Flood................................................... *68*
Hopewell ......................................................... *87*
Hornwork ................................................. *17, 28-29*
Horseshoe Creek .............................................. *70*
Howell Road .................................................... *87*
Hurricane Creek......................................*55, 68, 70*
Hurricane Creek Road ................................. *70, 88*
Hurst, Robert (Bob) .................. *17, 19, 25, 77, 99, 100*

### I

Itchetucknee River.................................... *36-39*
Ichetucknee Springs ....................... *38-39, 81, 83, 87*
Itoniah Scrub ............................................. *18, 36*

### J

Jackson, Andrew .........................*14, 22, 45, 64-65, 70, 74, 76, 78, 80, 85*
Jackson or Jackson's Trail .............*13, 17, 19, 22-24, 73*

Jackson Red Ground Florida Trail............ *76, 78, 86, 88*
Jacob Road .............................................. *19, 65-66, 87*
Jesus, Fray....................................................... *32*
Jones, Frank S. .............. *1, 17, 23, 33, 47, 53, 67-68, 89*

### K

Keith Cabin Historic Marker ..................... *83*
Keystone Heights .......................................... *87*
King's Road .................................................... *29*

### L

Lagino River .................................................... *54*
La Conception de Ayubale ............................. *50*
La Encarnation a la Santa Cruz de Sabacola .............. *60*
Lake Catherine ................................................ *57*
Lake Douglas Road .....................................*18, 55-56*
Lake Iamonia .............................................. *48, 50*
Lake Jackson, Leon County................................ *53-54*
Lake Jackson, Walton County .......................... *19, 24*
Lake Miccosukee ......................................... *46-47*
Lake Monteocha Creek ..................................... *36*
Lake Sampala ........................................... *43, 49*
Lake Sampala Road ......................................... *43*
Laurel Hill ............................................... *73, 88*
Lela ................................................................. *56*
Leon, Ponce de............................................... *21*
Letchworth-Love Mounds
Archaeological State Park.........................*18, 46, 83*
Limestone Branch .......................................... *68*
Limestone Creek ............................................ *58*
Little Attapulgus Creek ................................... *55*
Little Aucilla River............................................ *43*
Little River .............................................. *11, 22*
Little River Springs Conservation Area ................. *11, 39*
Littman .................................................... *60, 87*
Lockhart.......................................................... *88*
Lower Creek Indians ........................................ *73*
Lower Creek Trading Path ............ *19, 24, 67, 71, 73, 86*
Lower Path ........................................*11, 24, 45*

### M

Mahan Drive .................................................... *52*
Malapaz ..................................................... *1, 36*
Maria Branch ................................................... *77*
Marianna .............................................. *19, 57, 63-64*

| | |
|---|---|
| Marquez, Thomas Menendez | *36* |
| Mayo Junction | *87* |
| Melrose | *83* |
| Mendoza, Manuel de | *51* |
| Meridian Road | *52* |
| Miccosukee | *18, 22, 41, 45-48, 52* |
| Military Road | *34, 43* |
| Mill Creek | *36, 41* |
| Miller Crossroads | *88* |
| Milton | *74* |
| Mission Road | *17, 22, 24-25, 36-37, 100* |
| Mission San Carlos Interpretive Kiosk | *83* |
| Mission Spring | *38* |
| Mobile Bay | *80* |
| Mt. Ida Road | *68* |
| Mole Branch | *76* |
| Monteocha Creek | *32, 35* |
| Mount Pleasant, Floridatown | *73, 80* |
| Mount Pleasant, Gadsden Co. | *87* |
| Movila Indians | *80* |
| Muddy Branch | *76* |
| Munson Slough | *53* |
| Murder Creek | *74* |

### N

| | |
|---|---|
| Narvaez, Panfilo de | *41* |
| Natural Bridge Creek | *70* |
| Natural Bridge of the Chipola River | *57, 64-65* |
| Natural Bridge of the Santa Fe River | *25, 36-37* |
| Neal's Landing | *24* |
| New Harmony Road | *87* |
| New Hope | *88* |
| Newnansville | *25, 36* |
| NE 127th Street | *36* |
| NE 211 Drive | *37* |
| North Mosquito Creek | *60* |

### O

| | |
|---|---|
| Oak Grove | *87, 88* |
| Ocalquibe | *53* |
| Ochlocknee River | *11, 22, 54, 87* |
| Ococo | *43* |
| Okchai Indians | *68* |
| Okchiahatchee | *67* |
| Okiakhija | *53* |

| | |
|---|---|
| Old Bainbridge Road | *18, 53, 86-87* |
| Old Field Path | *18, 22-23, 45-48, 51* |
| Old Miccosukee Road | *52* |
| Old St. Augustine Road | *42, 50* |
| Old Spanish Road | *21, 25, 34, 81, 86-87* |
| Old Spanish Trail | *19, 21, 62, 81, 86-87, 99-100* |
| Oleno State Park | *18, 37-38, 83, 85, 87* |
| Orange Heights | *87* |

### P

| | |
|---|---|
| Pace | *19, 78, 88* |
| Palmetto Creek | *77* |
| Panther Creek | *76* |
| Paraner's Trail | *18, 37-28, 85* |
| Path to Deer Point | *68, 74* |
| Path to Latchua | *36* |
| Path to Lower Store | *36* |
| Path to Pea Creek | *70* |
| Path to the Tukabatchees | *73* |
| Path to Yellow Water | *70* |
| Peanut Road | *65, 87* |
| Pea Ridge | *88* |
| Pena, Diego | *13-14, 22, 29, 32, 36-37, 39-41, 49-50* |
| Pensacola | *13, 15, 17-19, 21, 24, 30, 32, 34-35, 41-42, 47, 52-54, 57-59, 70-71, 74, 79* |
| Pensacola Bay | *54, 68, 73, 89* |
| Pensacola or Penzacola Indians | *79-80* |
| Pensacola to Geneva Road | *81* |
| Pepayvitta | *36* |
| Picolata | *29, 40* |
| Picolata Path | *17, 22, 29* |
| Picolata Road | *17, 30* |
| Pine Lake | *43* |
| Pine Lake Road | *87* |
| Pine Log Creek | *70* |
| Pintado, Vincente Sebastian | *19, 59-60, 89* |
| Pittman | *88* |
| Pogee Creek | *36* |
| Pokanaweethly | *67* |
| Polley Creek | *75-76* |
| Pond Creek | *70, 78* |
| Prim Road | *65, 87* |
| Pupa | *30-31, 33* |
| Purcell, Joseph | *13-14, 21-22, 25, 30-31, 35, 37, 41-42, 45, 47, 51-52* |

## Q

| | |
|---|---|
| Quincy Creek | 60 |

## R

| | |
|---|---|
| Red Clay Creek | 76 |
| Reddoch Road | 19, 62-63, 87 |
| Red Ground Path | 18-19, 23-24, 57-58, 67-68, 70-71, 73, 81 |
| Rice Creek | 32 |
| Rio de Blanco | 32 |
| Rivera, Enrique Primo de | 33 |
| Road to Calistoble | 19, 23-24, 61, 66-67 |
| Road through Georgia | 18, 47, 55, 58 |
| Road to Sabacola | 22-23, 59 |
| Road to San Francisco | 36 |
| Rockarch | 66 |
| Rock Pond | 56 |
| Rocky Creek | 36 |
| Royals Crossroads | 88 |
| Royal Spring | 39, 83 |
| Rosworth, Sam | 17, 28 |
| Ruiz, Fray | 27 |
| Rum Road | 63 |
| Running Spring | 40 |

## S

| | |
|---|---|
| St. Augustine | 11, 13, 17-18, 21-22, 27-29, 30-31, 33-34, 57, 81, 83, 86 |
| St. Johns River | 13, 17, 27, 30-35, 38, 40 |
| St. Marks | 51 |
| St. Marks River | 29 |
| St. Sebastian River | 29 |
| Sabacola | 23, 59-60 |
| Salem Road | 55 |
| Sampala Swamp | 43 |
| San Carlos de Yatcatahi | 65 |
| San Cosme | 54 |
| San Damien Yecambi | 54 |
| San Francisco de Ocone | 50 |
| San Juan de Aspalaga | 50 |
| San Juan de Guacara | 18, 19, 40, 42 |
| San Juan River | 41, 74 |
| San Lorenzo de Ivitachucoso | 50 |
| San Luis Mission | 22, 52-54, 81, 87 |
| San Martin de Ayaocuto | 38 |
| San Martin de Timucua | 38 |
| San Matheo de Tolanatofi | 49 |
| San Miguel de Asile | 50 |
| San Nicholas | 60, 62, 65 |
| San Nicolas de Tolentino | 65 |
| San Pedro de Patale | 48-49, 61 |
| San Pedro Old Fields | 41-42 |
| San Pedro Path | 18, 22, 41-43, 47 |
| San Pedro y San Pablo de Potohiriba | 43 |
| San Marcos Mission | 22 |
| Santa Cruz de Sabacola Mission | 23, 60, 64 |
| Santa Cruz de Tarihica II | 39 |
| Santa Elena de Machava | 49 |
| Santa Fe Lake | 36 |
| Santa Fe River | 25, 35-38 |
| Santa Rosa de Ivitanayo | 35 |
| Scotland | 54, 87 |
| Seaboard Coast Railroad | 54-55 |
| Second Seminole War | 17-18, 30, 36 |
| Seminoles | 48 |
| Senetahago | 47 |
| Serenity Gardens | 88 |
| Shady Rest Road | 54-55, 59 |
| Sharon Road | 65, 87 |
| Shoal River | 74 |
| Shrine of the Martyrs | 83 |
| Sixmile Swamp | 29 |
| Smith Lake | 35 |
| Sneads | 62, 81, 83, 87 |
| Spring Creek | 47, 55-56, 67-68 |
| Spring Hill | 88 |
| Springhill Methodist Church | 83 |
| State Line Road | 67 |
| State Road 2 | 67, 67-68 |
| State Road 26 | 87 |
| State Road 21 | 36 |
| State Road 270 | 59 |
| Steadham, Benjamin | 68 |
| Steam Mill Road | 57 |
| Stokes Road | 73 |
| Sundown Creek | 43 |
| Sundown Creek Road | 87 |
| Sunray Road | 18, 46, 87 |
| Suwannee River | 11, 15, 18, 22, 38-42, 45, 99, 100 |
| Swan Lake | 36 |
| Sweet Water Creek | 77 |

## T

| | |
|---|---|
| Tagabona | *53* |
| Tallahassee Talofa | *52-53* |
| Tallahassee | *13, 15, 18, 21-22, 45, 52, 86, 87* |
| Tallapoosa River | *73* |
| Tanner Springs | *65* |
| Teller Road | *70* |
| Thomas Road | *73* |
| Ticosoriva | *43* |
| Toaputare | *52* |
| Tomatley | *62* |
| Tonaby | *53* |
| Toole Dairy Road | *18, 56* |
| Townsend Branch | *36* |
| Trading Path from the Head of Santa Rosa Bay to Ekanachattee | *57* |
| Trail Ridge | *32* |
| Traxler | *83, 87* |

## U

| | |
|---|---|
| Underground Creek | *70* |
| Union Church Road | *88* |
| Union Road | *19, 65, 87* |
| United States Arsenal | *83* |
| Upper Creek Indians | *73* |
| Upper Path | *22, 45-46* |
| Upper San Pedro Path | *22, 43, 47* |
| U. S. Highway 17 | *17* |
| U. S. Highway 19/27 | *45, 49, 86* |
| U. S. Highway 84 | *18* |
| U. S. Highway 90 | *42, 52, 60, 62, 81, 87* |
| U. S. Highway 98 | *18* |
| Usichua | *39* |
| Usiparachua | *39* |
| Usybitta | *41* |

## V

| | |
|---|---|
| Vega, Garcilaso de la | *50-52, 89* |
| Vignoles, Charles B. | *21, 89* |
| Wadesboro Road | *18, 52, 87* |
| Wallace Williams Pioneer Home | *83* |
| Weechatookamee Spring | *38* |
| Weeden Island Culture | *46* |
| Weehiheaga | *78* |
| Weekasupka (Creek) | *77* |
| Weekaywee Hatchee | *68* |
| Weelanee River | *74* |
| Weelustee (Creek) | *78* |
| Welaunee Creek | *50* |
| Wes Skiles Peacock Springs State Park | *18-19, 39, 83, 86* |
| West Bainbridge | *18, 56* |
| White, Joseph M. | *46* |
| White Sands Lake | *35* |
| White Sands Road | *87* |
| Willacoochee Creek | *55* |
| Willoughby Lane | *68* |
| Woodham Road | *68* |
| Wrights Creek | *68* |

## Y, Z

| | |
|---|---|
| Yamassee Indians | *80* |
| Yellow River | *19, 70, 74-76* |
| Yellow River Baptist Church Road | *19, 75* |
| Yellow Water Bay | *80* |
| Young, Hugh | *11, 14-45, 52-53, 64, 67, 70, 74-78, 80-89* |
| Yustaga | *43* |
| Zorn Road | *18, 56* |

www.ingramcontent.com/pod-product-compliance
Lightning Source LLC
Chambersburg PA
CBHW041452020526
44114CB00054B/78